POCKET DICTIONARY of THEOLOGICAL TERMS

STANLEY J. GRENZ,
DAVID GURETZKI &
CHERITH FEE NORDLING

InterVarsity Press
Downers Grove, Illinois

InterVarsity Press
P.O. Box 1400, Downers Grove, IL 60515
World Wide Web: www.ivpress.com
E-mail: mail@ivpress.com

InterVarsity Press® *is the book-publishing division of InterVarsity Christian
Fellowship/USA*®, *a student movement active on campus at hundreds of
universities, colleges and schools of nursing in the United States of America, and
a member movement of the International Fellowship of Evangelical Students. For
information about local and regional activities, write Public Relations Dept.,
InterVarsity Christian Fellowship/USA, 6400 Schroeder Rd., P.O. Box 7895,
Madison, WI 53707-7895.*

All Scripture quotations, unless otherwise indicated, are taken from the Holy
Bible, New International Version®. NIV®. *Copyright ©1973, 1978, 1984 by
International Bible Society. Used by permission of Zondervan Publishing House.
All rights reserved.*

Cover illustration: Roberta Polfus

ISBN 0-8308-1449-3

Printed in the United States of America ⊖

Library of Congress Cataloging-in-Publication Data
Grenz, Stanley, 1950-
    *Pocket dictionary of theological terms/Stanley J. Grenz, David
Guretzki, Cherith Fee Nording.*
      p.   cm.
    Includes bibliographical references (p.   ).
    ISBN 0-8308-1449-3 (pbk.: alk. paper)
    *1. Theology—Dictionaries.   I. Guretzki, David.   II. Nording,
Cherith Fee.   III. Title.*
    BR95.G66   1999
    230'.03—dc21   *99-18214*
                                                             CIP

17   16 15   14   13   12   11   10   9   8   7

12   11   10   09   08   07   06   05   04   03   02

Preface
A Note to the Reader

"You can't know the players without a scorecard!" claim the program vendors as they make their way through ballpark stands. In a similar manner we might say, "You can't understand theology without definitions."

This *Pocket Dictionary* attempts to provide a basic understanding of the three hundred or so significant words and concepts you are most likely to encounter in the theological books and articles you are reading. The entries consist primarily of English terms, but we also have included key foreign phrases—especially Latin and German—as well as a select group of theologians who have played central roles in the history of theology.

In using the *Pocket Dictionary* keep several things in mind. First, the format of the book is quite simple. The terms, phrases and names are arranged together in alphabetical order. Second, we have focused our attention on basic, generally held definitions. Rather than being exhaustive treatments, therefore, our descriptions seek to provide you with a foundational, working knowledge of the concepts. This working knowledge in turn ought to place you in a position to glean a fuller understanding from the theology texts you are reading, the lectures you are hearing or even the information you find in more exhaustive theological dictionaries. Third, while much of the material we present is generally accepted among the various Christian traditions, the fact that we write from a broadly evangelical, Protestant perspective is clearly evident from time to time.

The *Pocket Dictionary* is a reference book. Thus we do not intend that you read it from cover to cover. Rather we anticipate that you will have it next to you or on your desk as you read theological literature. You can then consult the *Pocket Dictionary* when you come across a term that is unfamiliar to you. If you are a student, you might also use it as a "crib sheet" to help you prepare for whatever definition-oriented exams you might encounter.

Being a reference book, the *Pocket Dictionary* is cross-referenced. An asterisk before a term or phrase indicates that it appears elsewhere in the book as a separate entry. *See* and *see also* references indicate entries that might provide additional information. Typical abbreviations found in reference works like the *Pocket Dictionary* include *c. (circa)* meaning "approximately," *b.* standing for "born" and *d.* meaning "died."

As members of Christ's church and disciples of Jesus we find reading theology highly rewarding. We hope you will too. And we hope that this *Pocket Dictionary* will assist you in the process.

The Authors

A

a posteriori, a priori. Terms used to refer to whether an assertion is dependent on experience (a posteriori) or independent of experience (a priori). For example, if one observes creation and sees in it an organized pattern, it might be concluded a posteriori (i.e., on the basis of observing creation) that God exists as its cause. However, if God's existence can be proved on some basis prior to sense experience, then the existence of God is argued a priori.

accommodation. Speaks of God making himself known to humans in words and ways suitable for the finite human mind to comprehend. The most significant example in which God accommodates to humankind is found in the coming of Jesus Christ—deity taking human form. *See also* incarnation.

adiaphora. Items of belief not essential to *salvation. In Lutheran thought the adiaphora were defined as practices of the church that were neither commanded nor forbidden in Scripture. In contemporary terms, adiaphora are those things not clearly addressed by Scripture that Christians may freely practice or believe with a clear conscience before God and that do not affect salvation.

adoption. God's act of making otherwise estranged human beings part of God's spiritual family by including them as inheritors of the riches of divine glory. This adoption takes place through our receiving in faith the work of Jesus Christ the Son (Jn 3:16), being born of the Spirit (Jn 3:5-6) and receiving the Spirit of adoption (Rom 8:15-16). *See also* reconciliation.

adoptionism. The theory that asserts that God adopted Jesus of Nazareth as his Son. In other words, Jesus was born human but became God's Son at a particular point in his life. This theory fails to reflect scriptural texts that point to Jesus' eternal relationship with the Father (e.g., Jn 17:5).

advent. Literally meaning "coming" or "arrival," this term refers to the coming of Jesus Christ to earth to provide *salvation by his life, death, resurrection and ascension. Christians now anticipate a second advent when Christ will return to earth in bodily form to receive the church and to judge the nations. The term *Advent* also refers to a season of the church year during which the church prepares to commemorate Christ's first coming to earth (Christmas). The Advent season encompasses the four Sundays prior to Christmas Day. *See also* parousia.

aesthetics (esthetics). The area of philosophy formally concerned with defining the nature of beauty and discovering criteria or standards by which something can be evaluated as beautiful. In Christian theology beauty is usually defined as what reflects in some way God's own character and nature. *See also* ethics.

agnosticism. Literally, "no knowledge" and taken from two Greek terms, *a* (no) and *gnosis* (knowledge). In a more formal sense *agnosticism* refers to a system of belief in which personal opinion about religious statements (e.g., "God exists") is suspended because it is assumed that they can be neither proven nor disproven or because such statements are seen as irrelevant. *See also* atheism.

Alexandrian school. So called because of its origin in the city of Alexandria (Egypt), this Christian center of scholarship was led first by Clement of Alexandria in A.D. 190 and then by *Origen in A.D. 202. The Alexandrian school was influenced by the philosophy of Plato and understood the task of biblical interpretation as seeking out its literal, moral and allegorical senses. In other words, the Alexandrian theologians taught that although the Bible was literally true, its correct interpretation lay in the moral or allegorical senses more than in the literal sense. *See also* Antiochene school.

allegory, allegorical method. An allegory is a story in which the details correspond to or reveal a "hidden," "higher" or "deeper" meaning. The allegorical method of biblical interpretation assumes that biblical stories should be interpreted by seeking the "spiritual" meaning to which the literal sense points. *See also* typology.

amillennialism. The belief that the thousand years mentioned in Revelation 20 do not represent a specific period of time between Christ's first and second comings. Many amillennialists believe instead that the *millennium refers to the heavenly reign of Christ and the departed saints during the Church Age. Amillennialists usually understand Revelation 20 to mean that the return of Christ will occur at the end of history and that the church presently lives in the final era of history. *See also* premillennialism; postmillennialism.

Anabaptist. A general term referring to several varied movements coming out of the Protestant *Reformation in the 16th century, often referred to as the *Radical Reformation. Anabaptists rejected infant baptism as practiced in the Lutheran and Reformed churches. Furthermore, Anabaptists believed that these churches either had been corrupted or had not separated themselves fully from what the Anabaptists considered to be errors of the Roman Catholic Church. Anabaptists therefore urged their followers to be baptized as conscious disciples of Christ. Significant Anabaptists include Menno Simons and Jacob Hutter. *See also* Mennonites.

analogy of being *(analogia entis).* The argument that there is sufficient similarity between God and creation so that observation of the universe will yield a limited understanding of God's nature. The analogy of being is usually said to extend more to humans than to the universe itself, in that humans are created in the image of God *(see imago Dei).* Contemporary theologians have debated the extent to which sinful humans can perceive creation as pointing to God. Some theologians (e.g., Karl *Barth) reject completely the use of the analogy of being as a valid theological principle.

analogy of faith *(analogia fidei).* A principle of interpretation that suggests that clearer passages of Scripture should be used to interpret more obscure or difficult passages. For *Augustine the analogy of faith requires that Scripture never be interpreted in such a way that it violates the church's summary of Christian faith (i.e., the Apostles' Creed). For Luther, Christ is the analogy of faith, so that Scripture needs always to be interpreted as testifying to Christ. For Calvin the analogy of faith assumes that because the Spirit oversaw its writing, Scripture and the Spirit together interpret other parts of Scripture.

analytical philosophy. An early twentieth-century philosophical movement that sought to understand how a sentence "means" something. Early analytical philosophers (e.g., A. J. Ayer) asserted that sentences are meaningful only if they can be verified or falsified in some way, at least theoretically. This suggests that religious, ethical and poetic sentences are meaningless, in that they can neither be verified nor falsified. *See also* logical positivism.

Anglican, Anglicanism. Anglicanism began in seventeenth-century England as part of the English Reformation and continues as the state church of England. Anglicanism was formed out of the theology of *Protestantism, especially *Calvinism, but maintained a strong affinity to the worship and structure of the Roman Catholic Church. Common to all of Anglicanism is its use of the *Book of Common Prayer in worship. It declares the central Anglican principle: "The rule of prayer is the rule of belief."

anhypostasis. The belief that Christ in his incarnation did not take characteristics of a specific human being upon himself, but rather took on humanity in a "generic" sense. Thus Jesus of Nazareth was not so much a "new" human as much as he was "like" a human in every way. Traditionally, the church has rejected the anhypostasis theory as an inadequate explanation of Christ's humanity.

animism. A system of belief that asserts that spirit beings are the cause of all movement, growth or change (animation) in the world. Although many animists acknowledge one most powerful god, they are highly sensitive to the presence of the spiritual in the world. Animists, therefore, would explain various movements, such as the growth of a tree, the rustling of its leaves and the shedding of its leaves, as visible effects of invisible spirits.

annihilationism. The belief that all the wicked will be judged by God and thrown into the lake of fire, where they will cease to exist. Some annihilationists suggest that this will occur instantaneously, while others believe that the unrighteous may experience a brief period of awareness. However, all annihilationists agree that no individual, however wicked, will suffer eternally a conscious existence in hell. *See also* conditional immortality.

Anselm of Canterbury (1033-1109). A medieval monk, philosopher and theologian who eventually became the archbishop of Canterbury, England. Anselm is best known for his formulation of the *ontological argument for the existence of God, as well as his *satisfaction theory of the atonement. Anselm also sought to understand the reasons that God had to become human in Christ and give himself as a sacrifice for sin. Anselm understood the task of theology as *fides quaerens intellectum* (faith seeking understanding).

anthropology. From the Greek words *anthrōpos* (human) and *logos* (word), that is, words about, or teaching concerning, humankind. Anthropology in general refers to any study of the status, habits, customs, relationships and culture of humankind. In a more specific and theological sense, anthropology sets forth the scriptural teachings about humans as God's creatures. Christian anthropology recognizes that humans are created in God's image *(*imago Dei)* but that sin has in some way negatively affected that image. Anthropology is also interested in the question of the constitution of a human being, that is, the relationship between body, soul, spirit and so on.

anthropomorphism. A figure of speech used by writers of Scripture in which human physical characteristics are attributed to God for the sake of illustrating an important point. For example, Scripture sometimes speaks of the "face" or "arm" of God, even though God is revealed to be Spirit and not limited in time and space by the constraints of a physical body. Anthropomorphisms essentially help to make an otherwise abstract truth about God more concrete.

antichrist. Literally, "against Christ," the term refers to individual, social or ideological opposition to the words and deeds of Christ. Some theologians understand the antichrist to be a future individual who will oppose Christ and whose rule in the world will serve as a sign of the nearness of Christ's second coming. The term appears only in the letters of John, yet biblical writers in both the OT and the NT used similar concepts, such as "sons of Belial" (as found in the Pentateuch and historical books); "the little horn" (Daniel); "the abomination of desolation" (Matthew and Mark, see Daniel); and the "man of lawlessness" (Paul).

antinomianism. An ethical system that denies the binding nature of any supposedly absolute or external laws on individual behavior. Some antinomianists argue that Christians need not preach or practice the laws of the OT because Christ's merits have freed Christians from the law. Others, like the early *Gnostics, teach that spiritual perfection comes about through the attainment of a special knowledge rather than by obedience to law. Generally, Christian theology has rejected antinomianism on the basis that although Christians are not saved through keeping the law, we still have a responsibility to live uprightly, that is, in obedience to God's law of love in service to one another (Gal 5:13-14) as we walk by the Spirit (Gal 5:16) who continually works to transform us into the image of Christ the Creator (Col 3:1, 7-10).

antinomy. The bringing together of two principles, statements or laws that, even though appearing to be contradictory to or in tension with one another, are both believed to be true. A theological example of an antinomy is the belief in both the absolute sovereignty of God and human free will. Although both are held to be true, there is a tension between God's will and our human will that cannot be easily or fully understood. *See also* paradox.

Antiochene school. So called because it arose in the city of Antioch in the third to fifth centuries A.D., the Antiochene school practiced an approach to scriptural interpretation that emphasized the literal meaning of the text. This was in reaction to the *Alexandrian school of interpretation, which sought "deeper" allegorical, moral or spiritual meanings not immediately evident in the text. Important figures in the Antiochene school include Chrysostom, Theodor, Theodoret and Theophilus. *See also* Alexandrian school.

apocalypse. From the Greek word meaning "unveiling." Its use as the title of the last book of the NT (the book of Revelation, or the Apocalypse) arises from John's opening phrase: *apokalypsis Iesou Christou* (Revelation of Jesus Christ).

apocalyptic literature, apocalypticism. Certain portions of the Bible (including Daniel 7—12 and the book of Revelation) are often categorized as *apocalyptic literature,* a genre or type of Jewish literature that became popular during the intertestamental period and extended into the NT era (c. 400 B.C. to A.D. 100). The writers of apocalyptic literature sought to disclose "heavenly secrets" concerning how the world would end and how the kingdom of God would suddenly appear to destroy the kingdom of evil. Apocalyptic writers made extensive use of visions, dreams and symbols as instruments of revealing what was hidden. *Apocalypticism* has been variously defined as a social movement or ideology arising out of an oppressed subgroup in a society, whether ancient or modern, which in defining its identity seeks release from oppression by seeing a future reality as more important than the present state of affairs.

apokatastasis. A Greek word loosely translated as "restoration." In the OT the Hebrew equivalent of the term referred to the return of Israel from exile (see Jer 16:15). In the NT *apokatastasis* speaks of a future time when God in Christ will restore all things in creation according to God's original intention. Some theologians have taken this to mean that at the end of history all humankind (and perhaps even Satan and his demons) will be saved. Generally, Christian theology has rejected the idea of a universal *salvation. *See also* universalism.

Apollinarianism, Apollinarius. The teaching of the fourth-century bishop of Laodicea Apollinarius (c. 310-391), who declared that in his incarnation Christ took on a human body and soul but not a human mind or spirit *(nous).* Apollinarius argued that to have a human spirit is to have a free will. But where there is free will, there is also sin. Therefore, Apollinarius concluded, Christ operated solely on the basis of a divine mind or *nous.* The church officially rejected Apollinarianism at the Second Ecumenical Council at Constantinople in A.D. 381.

apologetics. Occasionally called *eristics,* apologetics is the formal defense of the Christian faith. Historically, Christian theologians have differed as to whether apologetics is appropriate to the presentation of the gospel, and if so, how it should be accomplished. Depending on how they have answered these questions, apologists have appealed to rational argumentation, empirical evidence, fulfilled prophecy, authorities of the church or mystical experience in defending such beliefs as the existence of God, the authority of Scripture, the deity of Christ and the historicity of Jesus' resurrection. *See also* polemics.

apophatic theology. Generally, any kind of theology that assumes that positive description of God is impossible, for by definition God, as an uncreated being, does not fit into normal categories of human language and thought. As a result, apophatic theology is often called "negative theology" because it assumes that all that human language can do is assert what God is not—for example, that God is infinite (not finite), immutable (not changing), immortal (not mortal). As a result, apophatic theology suggests that God is known positively through spiritual experience rather than through rational expression. Apophatic theology is of key importance in the Eastern Orthodox tradition. *See also* Eastern Orthodoxy; *via eminentia, via negativa, via causalitatus.*

apostasy. A biblical concept that generally refers to those who fall away from belief in God. Broadly speaking, *apostasy* has been defined in four ways: as referring to a person who falls away and fails to keep a religious covenant (Judaism), who falls away from the church (Roman Catholicism), who falls away from intellectual adherence to Christianity (*Augustinianism/*Calvinism), or who falls away from *salvation once experienced (*Semi-Pelagianism/Arminianism). Scripture repeatedly and clearly warns of the dangers and results of apostasy (e.g., Heb 6:4-8).

apostle, apostolicity. Derived from the Greek term *apostolos,* an apostle is basically a "sent one." From his many followers Christ chose twelve whom he designated as "apostles" (Mt 10:2-4; Mk 3:14; Lk 6:14-16). These twelve, along with the apostle Paul as one "abnormally born" (1 Cor 15:8), became foundational in the establishment of the church and functioned as authority figures in the early church. As a result, the idea of *apostolicity* has to do with the correspondence of the faith and practice of the church to the authoritative NT teaching attributed to the apostles.

appropriation. A general term used in theology to speak of the integration or application of an aspect of the Christian belief system into Christian practice. Thus it is not enough to have an intellectual concept of faith and trust in Christ without actually exercising faith and trust in Christ. The believer's exercising of faith, then, is called the appropriation of faith.

Aquinas, Thomas (1225-1274). Medieval Italian theologian and monk whose work was declared to be the official teaching of the Roman Catholic Church by Pope Leo XIII in 1879. Aquinas's greatest influence is found in his *Summa Theologica,* a systematic presentation of Christian theology based on the philosophical system of Aristotle. One of his more famous contributions was a thorough discussion of the *Five Ways (proofs) for the existence of God.

Arianism, Arius. An early heretical teaching about the identity of Jesus Christ. Arianism was founded primarily on the teachings of Arius (d. 335/336). The central characteristic of Arian thought was that because God is one, Jesus could not have also been truly God. In order to deal with the scriptural testimony to the exalted status of Christ, Arius and his followers proposed that Jesus was the highest created being of God. So although Christ was fully human, he was not fully God. Arius's teaching was condemned as heretical at the First Ecumenical *Council (Nicaea) in A.D. 325.

Arminianism, Arminius. A system of theology founded on the thought of James Arminius (1560-1609), a Dutch theologian and pastor. Arminianism as a theological system developed mainly as a response to Lutheran and especially Calvinist views on the doctrine of *predestination. Unlike Calvinists (and Lutherans), who saw predestination as an unconditional action of God in electing individuals to *salvation, Arminius taught that predestination was based on God's foreknowledge in seeing whether an individual would freely accept or reject Christ. The resulting theology also asserted that insofar as *salvation is freely chosen, it could also be freely lost—a concept foreign to Calvinist and Lutheran understandings. *See also* Calvinism, John Calvin.

ascension. When Christ had finished his earthly ministry, he entered the presence of the Father (Mk 16:19; Lk 24:51; Acts 1:9). This event, known as the ascension, is significant for at least three reasons. First, the ascension ended the earthly, visible ministry of Christ and prepared the way for the promised coming of the Holy Spirit to minister invisibly through the church. Second, the ascension exalted Christ to the right hand of the Father, where he now reigns as Lord over the cosmos and serves as the great high priest, interceding on behalf of God's people (Heb 7:24; 8:2). Third, the ascension functions as a reminder that Christ will once again appear visibly from the heavens at his second coming (Acts 1:11).

asceticism. The teaching that spirituality is attained through renunciation of physical pleasures and personal desires while concentrating on "spiritual" matters. Jesus himself advocated certain practices such as fasting (Mt 9:15) or, for some perhaps, celibacy (Mt 19:12) for the sake of the kingdom; yet some Christians have overemphasized the role of ascetic practices. This prompted the apostle Paul to assert that ascetic practice alone is insufficient as a means of escaping from sin (see Col 2:20-23). Unfortunately, asceticism often proceeds on the assumption that the physical body is evil and is ultimately the cause of sin—a wholly unbiblical concept. *See also* Gnosticism.

aseity. A term derived from the Latin *a se,* "from oneself." *Aseity,* as a divine attribute, refers to God's self-existence. In other words, God is not dependent upon anything else for existence but has eternally existed without any external or prior cause.

assensus. A Latin term referring to the intellectual assent to or acceptance of a theological truth. While the biblical concept of faith includes the idea of *assensus,* it should not be equated with saving faith. One who exercises biblical faith assents to the truth that Jesus is both human and divine; however, *assensus* does not guarantee that biblical faith is present, for, as James notes, "even the demons believe" (Jas 2:19); that is, they give intellectual assent while not exercising saving faith in Christ. *See also* faith; fiducia; notitia.

assumption of Mary. A teaching originating in Roman Catholic thought during the medieval period that suggests that on her death Mary was transported (assumed), body and soul, into the heavenly presence of God. This doctrine was upheld by Pope Pius

XII in 1950 as an official Roman Catholic *dogma. There is no scriptural substantiation for this teaching, however. Non-Roman Catholic theologians therefore generally reject it. *See also* immaculate conception.

assurance. The doctrine that teaches the possibility of Christians' knowing that they truly are children of God. The apostle John teaches that assurance comes both as a result of living an obedient Christian life (1 Jn 2:3-6) and through the abiding presence and inner testimony of the Holy Spirit (1 Jn 4:13).

Athanasius (c. 296-373). An early church apologist, theologian and bishop of Alexandria. Athanasius's greatest contribution to Christian theology was his uncompromising stance against the popular Arian teaching of his day. *See also* Arianism, Arius.

atheism. A system of belief that asserts categorically that there is no God. Atheism usually affirms as well that the only form of existence is the material universe and that the universe is merely the product of chance or fate. *See also* agnosticism.

atonement, atonement theories. *Atonement* refers to God's act of dealing with the primary human problem, sin. Both OT and NT affirm that sin has broken the relationship between God and humankind. According to Christian theology, God accomplished the way of restoration through Christ's death. Although Scripture does not clearly spell out how this atonement takes place, some of the atonement theories include: (1) *moral influence—Christ's death acts as a positive example of love in action; (2) *ransom *(Christus victor)*— Christ is the ransom that buys back sinners from Satan or gains the victory over evil; (3) *satisfaction— Christ's death appeased the honor due God that has been robbed by human sin; and (4) *penal substitution— Christ stood in the legal place of sinners, bearing the just punishment due us because we transgress God's laws.

attribute, attributes of God. In general, an attribute is a characteristic or quality used to describe an object or person. When speaking of the attributes of God, theologians note those characteristics or qualities that are essential to our understanding of God as God relates to us as created beings. The attributes that classical Christian theology sets forth include *holiness, *eternality, *omniscience (all knowing), *omnipotence (all powerful), *omnipresence (present to all) and goodness. Some theologians would argue that love is an attribute of God, while others suggest that love is more closely related to God's essential being.

Augsburg Confession. Formulated in 1530, the Augsburg Confession summarizes the faith claims of Lutherans regarding Christ and his word. The Confession was written by Philipp Melanchthon, a devoted follower of Martin Luther. The Augsburg Confession has twenty-eight articles on topics such as God, humanity, sin, *salvation, the church and the end of the ages.

Augustine, Augustinianism (354-430). One of the greatest theologians in the history of the church, Augustine was influential in the development of the Western church's understanding of the doctrines of the *Trinity, sin, *predestination and the church. Augustine is known for his integration of the thought categories of Platonic philosophy with theology. Augustinianism as a system of thought essentially starts with the complete sinfulness of humankind (depravity), which leaves humans unable to respond in faith toward God. In keeping with this, Augustinianism asserts that God predestines those who are enabled to repent and believe.

axiology. An area of philosophical inquiry that studies the nature, criteria, implications and applications of value judgments. Generally, axiology asks, What is good (value theory)? What is right (*ethics)? and What is beautiful (*aesthetics)?

B

baptism. The practice of sprinkling with, pouring on or immersing in water as an act of Christian initiation and obedience to Christ's own command. Baptism as a Christian *ordinance or *sacrament is nearly universal in application throughout the Christian church, although there is great diversity in whether it is applied solely to those who consciously exercise faith in Christ (believer's baptism) or whether it is also to be extended to the infants of

Christian parents (infant baptism, or *pedobaptism).

baptismal regeneration. The belief that water baptism effects the saving work of the Holy Spirit in washing away original sin. In Roman Catholicism baptism (usually of infants) is understood to confer grace upon the individual, whether or not faith is present. In Lutheran theology baptism must be accompanied by faith, whether the faith of the individual or of the parents, to be effective in washing away sin. Other Protestants reject baptismal regeneration, arguing that it contradicts the concept of justification by grace through faith alone.

Barth, Karl (1886-1968). One of the most influential twentieth-century theologians, Karl Barth is often credited with being the father of *neo-orthodoxy or *dialectical theology. Barth is known for three main contributions. First, he emphasized the absolute *transcendence of God, contrary to liberals who emphasized God's *immanence. Second, he understood truth to arise out of the clash of opposing ideas—finite with infinite, eternity with time, God with humans. Finally, he placed Christ at the center of his theology, thus reversing the human-centered liberal theology that preceded him.

Basil (the Great) of Caesarea (c. 330-379). Basil, bishop of Caesarea, was one of three theologians known as the *Cappadocian fathers. Although influential in the rise of communal monasticism based on obedience, holiness and love, Basil is best remembered for his contribution to the development of the orthodox doctrine of the *Trinity. In his defense of the trinitarian faith, Basil introduced the formula for the Trinity as being one substance *(ousia)* and three persons *(hypostases)*.

believers' church. A theological conviction arising out of the *Radical Reformation that emphasizes the church as comprising only those who through faith in Jesus Christ voluntarily gather together for the sake of worship, instruction and doing good deeds. Contrary to the Augustinian view, proponents of the believers' church reject any definition of the church as a mixed body of believers and unbelievers. As a result, the believers' churches tend to focus on the local congregation as the community of those who are truly disciples of Jesus (the "gathered church").

biblical criticism. The method or methods by which meanings of biblical texts are sought through the application of techniques used in interpreting various types of literature. These methods include textual criticism, *redaction criticism, form criticism, *historical criticism, *genre criticism, literary criticism and grammatical criticism.

biblical theology. Biblical theology is the discipline that attempts to summarize and restate the teaching of a biblical text or of a biblical author without imposing any modern categories of thought on the text. Rather, the goal is to understand the "theology" of a biblical book or author in its original historical context. Many theologians see the work of biblical theology as logically prior to the task of *systematic theology, which attempts to state the biblical teaching in ways that address contemporary concerns.

biblical theology movement. Though biblical theology as a discipline traces its roots to the work of Johann Philipp Gabler (1753-1826), the biblical theology movement arose in the middle of the twentieth century as biblical scholars attempted to grapple with the authority of the text as well as to find an internal unity within the diversity of the biblical text. Some in the movement saw the Bible as a human book that was to be studied using methods common to the study of any other literature (*historical-critical method), while others continued to uphold the divine authority of Scripture and sought to understand the Bible as a theological book. Although the heyday of the biblical theology movement is past, the effects of the movement continue as a scholarly and pastoral discipline that seeks to uncover the message of Scripture for today's audience.

bibliology. The topic in *systematic theology that deals with issues of the nature and character of the Bible. Bibliology attempts to understand what kind of book the Bible is, how it is authoritative for Christian faith and practice, and to what extent and in what manner the Bible is to be understood as divine revelation.

binitarianism. A theory that affirms that God is to be understood as two persons sharing a single *essence or substance. Most binitarians affirm the personality of God the Father and God the Son, but usually define the Spirit of God as either a characteristic (or impersonal power) of the Father or Son, or as the action of God the Father and God the Son toward creation. *See also* trinitarianism.

blessed hope. The biblical phrase used to refer to the second coming of Christ as the fulfillment of our longings (see Tit 2:13). The main twentieth-century *evangelical-fundamentalist debate surrounding the blessed hope is whether it will be a secret appearing only to Christians prior to a period of great *tribulation (the *rapture anticipated by dispensational pretribulational *pre-millennialism) or whether Christ's appearance will be a public event observable by all people, whether Christian or not (most other eschatological positions, including *amillennialism, *post-millennialism and historic premillennialism).

Book of Common Prayer. The standard service and prayer book (*liturgy) used by the Church of England and Anglican/Episcopal communions throughout the world. The document was originally the work of Thomas Cranmer but has seen numerous revisions since its first publication in 1549. *See also* Anglican, Anglicanism.

Bonhoeffer, Dietrich (1906-1945). A German theologian who became involved in resistance to the Nazi government during World War II. Bonhoeffer was eventually executed as a war criminal in a German concentration camp. He is credited with several unique ideas that have entered common theological consciousness. These include "cheap grace," "religionless Christianity" and "the world come of age." Unfortunately, Bonhoeffer did not live long enough to complete his work, and thus there is some debate over what he meant by such phrases.

Brunner, Emil (1889-1966). A highly influential Swiss theologian who, along with Karl Barth, is associated with the movement called *neo-orthodoxy or *dialectical theology. Brunner rejected liberal theology's portrait of Jesus Christ as merely a highly respected human being. Instead Brunner insisted that Jesus was God incarnate and central to *salvation. Brunner also attempted to find a middle position within the ongoing *Arminian and *Calvinist debate, stating that Christ stood between God's sovereign approach to humankind and our free acceptance of God's gift of salvation. Though Brunner rightly reemphasized the centrality of Christ, conservative theologians have often been hesitant to accept Brunner's other teachings, including his rejection of certain "miraculous" elements of the Scriptures and his questioning of the usefulness of the doctrine of the inspiration of Scripture.

Bultmann, Rudolf (1884-1976). As professor at the University of Marburg, Germany, Bultmann was one of the most significant NT scholars of the twentieth century. He was a pioneer of the form-critical *(Formgeschichte)* approach to the Gospels, an approach that sought to discover the underlying oral sayings and events in the early church that eventually led to the actual text of the Gospels. He is also known for "demythologizing," that is, the attempt to identify the ancient "myths" assumed by the biblical authors and to translate these into modern terms. For Bultmann, this meant interpreting the NT using the categories developed by existentialist philosopher Martin Heidegger. For example, Bultmann restated the "primitive ideas" of sin as "inauthentic existence" and *salvation as "authentic existence."

Byzantine. Having to do with the ancient Greek city of Byzantium (renamed Constantinople in A.D. 330), which fell to invading Islamic armies in 1453. Byzantine theology evidenced a distinctively Eastern theological flavor. Byzantine theologians emphasized *salvation as "deification" in contrast to the Western view of salvation as a judicial transaction. Byzantine theology was also committed to reiterating the traditions of the patristic thinkers. Increasingly, Byzantine theologians saw themselves as maintaining the true faith in the face of the novel ideas of the Western tradition.

C

call (general, special, effectual). The act by which God extends to humans an invitation to enter into a saving relationship. The idea of a "general" call arises from scriptural texts that suggest that God's invitation goes out to all peoples through the testimony of general revelation, that is, as present in God's handiwork and providential care for creation. The "special" call refers to the Spirit of God working specifically in the heart of an individual as the preaching of the gospel provides the person with an opportunity to exercise faith in Christ. Finally, the "effectual" call refers to the Spirit's application of grace such that an individual receives forgiveness of sin and eternal life (*salvation).

Calvinism, John Calvin. The theological system of thought stemming from the work of one of the Reformation's greatest theologians and biblical scholars, John Calvin (1509-1564). Central to Calvin's thought, especially as seen in his *Institutes of the Christian Religion,* was the *sovereignty of God. Calvinism became a historical development of Calvin's thought as laid out in the *Institutes.* The *Synod of Dort (1618-1619) set forth what has become the standard summary of the major tenets of Calvinism. These are captured in the acronym TULIP (total *depravity, unconditional *election, *limited atonement, *irresistible grace and the *perseverance of the saints). *See also* Arminianism, Arminius.

canon. Literally meaning "standard" or "rule," the term is most closely associated with the collection of books that the church has recognized as the written Word of God (Scripture) and that functions as the rule or standard of faith and practice in the church. Although the various Christian traditions are not in full agreement as to which books should comprise the collection of Scripture, at the very least all agree that the sixty-six books of the Protestant Bible are canonical and therefore authoritative.

canonical criticism. An approach used to interpret the Bible in light of its final form as a theologically unified collection of books rather than seeking to understand the books in their precanonical form and function. Two of the most significant pioneers of canonical criticism as a modern interpretative approach are Brevard S. Childs and James Sanders. *See also* biblical criticism; criticism.

Cappadocian fathers. A group of theologians writing between the *Council of Nicaea (A.D. 325) and the *Council of Constantinople (A.D. 381). The Cappadocian fathers responded to the

Arian heresy and formulated the orthodox doctrine of the *Trinity. The group included *Basil of Caesarea (c. 330-379), *Gregory of Nyssa (c. 330-395) and *Gregory of Nazianzus (c. 330-389). The Cappadocian fathers' trinitarian formula stated that God is "three persons *[hypostaseis]* in one *essence *[ousia]*." *See also* Arianism, Arius.

casuistry. The attempt to formulate universal ethical rules or standards that can be applied in specific situations in order to ensure moral behavior. Casuistry, in other words, is the attempt to make general rules that can govern particular ethical issues.

catechesis, catechism. The process of teaching the basic Christian beliefs and the contents of the Scriptures either to a child who is raised in the church or to a new convert to Christianity. This process is often accomplished through the use of a *catechism,* a popular manual that often uses a question-and-answer format.

catholic. A term literally meaning "universal" or "worldwide." The word is most often associated with Roman Catholicism but originally became standardized in Christian theology through the formula appearing in early Christian creeds that affirms belief in "one holy catholic and apostolic church." To affirm the church's catholicity is to suggest that the church is universal in scope. In other words, the church is not restricted to any one ethnic group or geographical location but is open to Jew and Greek, slave and free, male and female (Gal 3:28), with its gospel message being directed to "all nations."

causality. A term derived from the closely related ideas of cause and effect. In theology, causality as a method seeks to determine the nature and attributes of God by seeking to identify and understand effects present in the world that are assumed to have been ultimately caused by God. In short, the method of causality assumes that there are marks left in creation that point to the ultimate cause, God as Creator.

Chalcedonian formula. The theological conclusion of the Ecumenical Council held in Chalcedon (A.D. 451), which attempted to delineate the relationship between Christ's humanity and his deity. The church accepted the Chalcedonian formula as the orthodox statement about the person of Christ. This formula confesses "one and the same Christ, Son, Lord, Only-begotten, made known in two natures without confusion, without change, without division, without separation, the difference of the natures being by no means removed because of the union [of the divine and the human]."

charismatic, charismatic movement. *Charismatic* literally means having to do with the *charismata,* or "gifts," of the Holy Spirit as delineated in several Pauline texts. In a general sense anyone who is part of the body of Christ, the church, and who exercises any gift of the Spirit may be said to be charismatic. However, in the mid-twentieth century a movement arose that emphasized the practice of the "sign" gifts (such as speaking in tongues, healing and miracles) and an emphasis on the "baptism of the Spirit" as an experience subsequent to *conversion. Although the charismatic movement began in a mainline Protestant context, it quickly became an interdenominational phenomenon affecting nearly all branches of Christianity, including Roman Catholicism and to a lesser extent *Eastern Orthodoxy.

chiliasm. *See* millennium, millennialism.

Christ, Christology. The Greek word translated in English as "Christ" is the equivalent of the Hebrew term *Messiah* and means "anointed one." Although not intrinsic to its meaning, the NT use of the term *Christ* tends to point to the deity of Jesus. Christology is the theological study devoted to answering two main questions: Who is Jesus? (the question of his identity) and What is the nature and significance of what Jesus accomplished in the incarnation? (the question of his work).

Christocentrism. The intentional or unintentional situating of Jesus Christ as the central or dominant theme of Christian theology. Christianity is christocentric by its very definition: Christians are those who follow Christ. However, Martin Luther, Karl Barth and Dietrich Bonhoeffer are examples of theologians who intentionally sought to develop their theology around Christ as either the starting point or the "standard" by which other theological concepts are understood and evaluated. In a negative sense, Christocentrism can lead to the neglect of the trinitarian aspects of the Christian faith, thus ignoring or downplaying the role of the Father and the Spirit.

church. A word generally used to translate the generic Greek word *ekklēsia,* which variously means "gathering," "assembly" or "congregation." However, the NT tends to use the word to refer to all those who by faith in the person and work of Christ as the fullest revelation of God have entered into a new relationship with God and with one another (1 Cor 1:9-10), who are the dwelling place of the Holy Spirit on earth (1 Cor 3:16) and who have been given the task of proclaiming the present and future reign of God in the world, both by the verbal declaration of the word of God (Acts 20:25-27) and by the administration of the *ordinances or *sacraments (Mt 28:19; 1 Cor 10:16-17). The church is founded on the past work of Christ in his death, resurrection and ascension, points to the return of Christ in the future and seeks to live in love by the power of the Spirit in the present.

circumcision. The practice of cutting off the foreskin of the male sexual organ. Originally, the practice was instituted by God (toward Abraham), and it became the external act signifying entrance into the OT community of faith. The Mosaic law prescribed that every Jewish male was to be circumcised on the eighth day after birth. Circumcision was also performed on Gentile proselytes (converts) to Judaism. According to the NT, through Christ external physical circumcision has been superseded by a spiritual "circumcision of the heart" (Rom 2:29).

circumincession. The theological concept, also referred to as perichoresis, affirming that the divine *essence is shared by each of the three persons of the *Trinity in a manner that avoids blurring the distinctions among them. By extension, this idea suggests that any essential characteristic that belongs to one of the three is shared by the others. Circumincession also affirms that the action of one of the persons of the Trinity is also fully the action of the other two persons.

clergy. Those persons who have been selected, set apart and acknowledged by the church to proclaim the Word of God and to administer the *ordinances or *sacraments. In certain Christian traditions such as Roman Catholicism, *Eastern Orthodoxy and some Reformed circles, the clergy hold a special authoritative status vis-à-vis nonclergy (*laity). In other traditions, especially in the various *believers' churches, clergy are seen as only functionally distinct from other Christians. That is, clergy carry out a special function in the church but do not have a higher status of authority than the laity.

coherence theory of truth. A theory of knowledge that asserts that a given proposition or statement is true when it is consistent within a larger set of propositions also taken to be true. If propositions come into conflict (are contradictory), it is assumed that either one or both of the propositions is false. The weakness of the coherence theory is that there can be no proof of the "starting point" or the "first proposition" of a belief system; instead, such a system of beliefs is usually accepted on the basis that it is self-evidently true.

coinherence. *See* circumincession.

communicatio idiomatum, communicatio operationum. *Communicatio idiomatum* is Latin for "communication of attributes." According to this teaching, Jesus' status as both fully God and fully human implies that whatever is true of Jesus' humanity is also true of his deity and vice versa without mixing the qualities of the divine or human nature. For example, if Jesus suffers and if Jesus is God, then it can be concluded that in Jesus God suffers. *Communicatio operationum* (communication of operations) suggests that any work or action of Christ's divine nature is at the same time the work of his human nature and vice versa. In short, both of these terms are meant to safeguard the fact that Jesus is only one person rather than two, even though the one person is both human and divine. Thus whatever Christ does is in fact the singular action of the one God-man.

communion. Generally, a term most closely related to the biblical idea of fellowship (from Greek *koinōnia*). It can refer to either the relational fellowship persons may have with God or the fellowship persons have with one another, especially with those who are in Christ. The term is also used in reference to the *Lord's Supper as an event marking the fellowship of the participants with Christ and with each other.

compatibilism. The theory that human free will is consistent (compatible) with God's sovereign prerogative to determine or will all things that are to happen. In order for this to be true, compatibilists usually argue that human freedom is only analogous to God's freedom and not identical with it. More specifically, human freedom is limited, whereas God's freedom is absolute.

concomitance. In Roman Catholic theology, the belief that Christ is physically present in the eucharistic elements of bread (which is his body) and wine (which is his blood). The doctrine of concomitance was eventually used to prevent the *laity from partaking of the wine in case it should be accidentally spilled, thus desecrating Christ himself.

concupiscence. A word that describes the fallen human tendency or strong desire toward engaging in sin. Concupiscence does not imply that humans will *always* fall into sin but simply that humans will desire sin even if they choose not to engage in it.

concurrence (*concursus divinus*). A term referring to any theory that attempts to define the relationship between the divine sovereignty of God and the free actions and responsibilities of created human beings. In particular, concurrence traditionally refers to the idea that God concurs with human wills in the acts that humans do.

conditional immortality. The belief that the human soul's eternal existence is dependent on God's gracious act of sustaining it. Those who hold to conditional *immortality suggest that the human soul is given eternal life only as a gift and that those who do not receive the gift of eternal life (the unsaved) will cease to exist sometime after death, either immediately or at the final judgment. *See also* annihilationism.

confession, confessionalism. A biblical concept related to the Greek *homologeō*, which means "to say the same thing" or "to agree," *confession* is used in a least three senses: (1) to acknowledge the greatness of God in praise and worship, (2) to acknowledge and repudiate sin, and (3) to verbalize basic doctrinal commitments. It is in this third sense of the term that confessions of faith—that is, doctrinal summaries of essential Christian beliefs—have been developed throughout the history of the Christian church. *Confessionalism* is the practice of doing theology within the context of a particular confession of faith, which is usually denominationally specific.

confirmation. According to Roman Catholicism and *Eastern Orthodoxy, confirmation is one of the *sacraments of the church and is administered by a clergyperson to children prior to receiving their first communion at about age twelve. This act gives a special grace to the child, enabling growth in faith. In certain Protestant traditions where infant (*see* pedobaptism) baptism is practiced, confirmation is a rite administered to children, usually around age thirteen, to allow them to formally affirm the baptism they received as infants.

congregationalism. A system of church government that assumes that Christ's authority comes directly to the local congregation. As a result, decisions in matters of faith and practice arise primarily if not solely out of the local congregation's corporate reading of Scripture. Today most congregationalism is "democratic" in the sense that the will of the majority of the people in the congregation constitutes what the local church believes and practices, and determines who should serve as its leaders.

consubstantiation. The theory of the *Lord's Supper most closely associated with the *Lutheran tradition. Martin Luther taught that the body and blood of the Lord is present "in, with and under" the actual bread and wine. This was in contrast to the Roman Catholic teaching of *transubstantiation, which taught that the bread and wine were transformed into the real body and blood of Jesus upon their consecration by the presiding priest.

consummation. Generally refers to either the completion of an era of God's working in history or the absolute completion of history (the final consummation). Most theologians see Christ's second coming as a definite act of consummation, whether that consummation entails the establishment of an earthly millennial kingdom (as in *premillennialism) or the completion of history itself (as in *postmillennialism and *amillennialism).

contextualization. The process of seeking to communicate the message and teachings of the ancient Scriptures using contemporary forms of language as well as metaphors and images that are familiar to the current audience. Contextualization raises the question as to how far a theologian may go in altering the language of Scripture without losing the *essence of the gospel message. Contextualization is also an attempt to understand ways in which the Christian community lives out the gospel in the midst of a non-Christian culture.

contingency. In philosophy, any event or object that is dependent on another event or object for it to happen or exist. This is in contrast to a *necessary* event or object, which happens or exists independently of other events and objects. For example, many philosophers argue that every object and event in creation is contingent, in contrast to God, who is a necessary being because by definition God is eternal and therefore *must* exist.

conversion. A general term referring to an individual's initial encounter with God in Christ resulting in the reception of God's gracious provision of *salvation. Some of the changes brought about in conversion include a change in heart from being dead in sin to being alive in Christ (*regeneration, Jn 1:12-13), a change in status from being guilty before God to being not guilty (*justification, Rom 3:21-31), a change in relationship from being an outcast and enemy to being a child and friend of God (*adoption and *reconciliation, 1 Jn 3:1; Col 1:20). Conversion begins the journey of discipleship through which a person who once was a slave to sin is being freed by the Holy Spirit for holiness (*sanctification).

coredemptrix. In contemporary Roman Catholic theology, the idea that Mary the mother of Jesus uniquely participated in the provision of *redemption, because she obediently became the mother of Christ in his incarnation and cosuffered in his passion by co-offering Christ to the Father as a redemptive sacrifice. Catholic theologians who argue for Mary as coredemptrix are usually careful to note that this status does not make Mary equal to Christ; yet they do suggest that redemption was accomplished by Christ with the free participation of Mary.

correspondence theory of truth. A theory of knowledge that asserts that a proposition is true when it corresponds to or harmonizes with an external reality "as it really is." One of the weaknesses of correspondence theory is that it is difficult to mediate between two or more differing conceptions of observed reality. In addition, it casts human knowledge in the form of measurable, observable qualities that supposedly inhere in the world.

cosmological argument. Any argument that attempts to demonstrate the existence of God by appeal to observation of the world (Greek *kosmos*), its objects and its processes. For example, Thomas *Aquinas argued that everything that moves points to something else moving it. Hence for every movement there must be a prior mover. Aquinas asserted that tracing this causal chain leads eventually to a First Mover that is unmoved. This Unmoved Mover, Aquinas concluded, is God.

cosmology. Derived from the Greek word *kosmos* (world), *cosmology* refers to the attempt to understand the origin, nature and subsequent history of the universe. Cosmology is an area where theology and science intersect, insofar as both are interested in understanding whether or not there is a first cause to the universe and whether or not there is purposeful direction and design in the universe.

Councils of Nicaea, Constantinople, Chalcedon. In several *ecumenical (i.e., including representation from all parts of the church) gatherings in the early centuries of the Christian history, church leaders discussed major theological issues for the purpose of coming to consensus on what the faithful should believe. The Council of Nicaea (A.D. 325) met primarily to resolve the debate over *Arianism (the doctrinal teaching that Christ was the highest created being) and concluded with the formulation of the anti-Arian *Nicene Creed. The Council of Constantinople (A.D. 381) extended the discussion to the identification of the Spirit within the Godhead, making the Creed fully trinitarian. Constantinople expanded the Nicene Creed and officially condemned Arianism as well as several other teachings, and it solidified the orthodox doctrine of the full humanity of Jesus Christ. The Council of Chalcedon (A.D. 451) focused on the relationship of Christ's humanity to his divinity and issued the formula of Chalcedon, which became the orthodox statement on the person of Christ. *See also* Chalcedonian formula.

Council of Trent (1545-1563). A theological council held by the Roman Catholic Church to respond to the challenges put forward by the theology of Martin Luther and other Protestant Reformers. The Council of Trent, which spanned the office of five popes, attempted to counter the Protestant doctrines of *justification, the *sacraments and Scripture.

covenant, covenant theology. *Covenant* refers to the act of God in freely establishing a mutually binding relationship with humankind. Through the covenant God bestows blessings on humans in conditional and unconditional terms. Conditionally, God blesses humans as they obey the terms of the covenant. Unconditionally, God bestows blessings on humans regardless of their obedience or disobedience to the terms of the covenant. God made covenants with Noah, Abraham, Moses and David. But above all, God has fulfilled these covenants and has inaugurated the New Covenant in Christ, which is for all people who trust in him (Heb 9:15, 27-28). Covenant theology is the system of theology that centers on God as a covenant-making God and sees in the history of creation two great covenants: the covenant of works and the covenant of grace. Covenant theology asserts that prior to the *Fall God made a covenant of works with Adam as the representative of all humankind. In response to Adam's disobedience God established a new covenant through the second Adam, Jesus Christ. Those who place their faith in Christ come under the benefits of this new covenant of grace. *See also* federal theology.

creatio ex nihilo. A Latin phrase that literally means "creation out of nothing." *Augustine is credited with developing the argument that God created the world without any preexisting materials. This was in contrast to most Greek philosophers, who understood the creative act as God's ordering of eternally existing materials into the present world or universe. The value of the doctrine of *creatio ex nihilo* is that it maintains a clear distinction between God and the created order and also maintains that God alone has eternal status.

creation. Christian theology views creation (entailing everything that exists other than God) as a result of God's spoken word. The

Christian doctrine of creation affirms that God is not to be equated with the universe (*pantheism), nor does God become inseparably bound to it (*panentheism). Instead, God remains completely distinct from the universe (*transcendence) while at the same time being intimately involved with it (*immanence). A biblical view of creation includes both the physical realm (the realm of objects, animals and people) and the spiritual realm (angels and demons).

creationism. In Christian anthropology, *creationism refers to the theory that God creates a person's soul directly. This is in contrast to the position that views the soul as eternally existing with God and also in contrast to *traducianism, which suggests that both the body and the soul are derived from one's parents. Creationism (or creation science) can also refer to a theory of the creation of the universe as having been accomplished in a literal seven-day week as recorded in the first chapters of Genesis. Many contemporary proponents of creation science also argue for a relatively young earth (usually younger than 50,000 years, or even under 10,000 years).

credo ut intelligam, credo quia absurdum. *Credo ut intelligam* translates literally, "I believe in order that I might understand." The phrase comes from *Anselm in his work *Proslogion I* and indicates his understanding of the relationship of faith to reason, namely, that faith is logically and chronologically prior to understanding and that it is through faith that understanding comes. *Credo quia absurdum* translates "I believe because it is absurd" and is credited to *Tertullian. For Tertullian, faith and reason are incompatible, and therefore faith entails belief in the unbelievable or the absurd.

creed. Derived from the Latin *credo* (I believe), a creed is a summary statement of Christian faith and belief. The purpose of the earliest creeds was to present a short summary of Christian doctrine, which baptismal candidates affirmed at their baptism. Later, creeds become tools for instruction of new converts, for combating heresy and for use in corporate worship. Three of the most famous creeds established in the first five centuries of church history are the Apostles' Creed, the *Nicene (or Niceno-

Constantinopolitan) Creed and the Athanasian Creed.

criticism (biblical, canonical, form, redaction). A term used in reference to any method of interpreting texts that uses modern scientific insights into the nature of history, language, culture and literature. More specifically, *biblical criticism is the attempt to interpret the Scriptures by uncovering the original meaning of the text, looking to the original historical setting in which it was written without reference to later theological traditions. In contrast, *canonical criticism is the attempt to interpret the Bible in light of the final form of Scripture as a theologically unified collection of books rather than seeking to understand the books in their precanonical form and function. Form criticism *(Formgeschichte)* is the attempt to go back to the original sources lying behind the text prior to its written form, such as by uncovering oral traditions and layers of material added to the scriptural say-ings in the process of oral tradition. *Redaction criticism is the attempt to identify the ways in which the writer or editor (e.g., Gospel writer) utilized sources in composing a biblical book in order to understand the author's theology and setting.

D

damnation. As a synonym for the final *judgment, *damnation* refers to the eternal condemnation of God on those who, because of their sinfulness, will not enter God's eternal kingdom but will suffer the eternal consequences of separation from God. Scripture also acknowledges that Satan and his rebellious demonic followers will suffer damnation for their acts of unrighteousness.

Day of the Lord. A biblical phrase prevalent among OT prophets who pointed to a future event or era (not necessarily a single twenty-four-hour day) during which God would visit *judgment on Israel or the world. The NT authors interpreted the phrase in a futuristic sense but saw in Jesus Christ the beginning of the fulfillment of the Day of the Lord. For believers in Christ the Day of the Lord is an anticipation of hope; for unbelievers it holds only judgment leading to *damnation.

deacon, deaconess. Derived from the Greek *diakoneō* (to serve), deacons (male and female) and deaconesses (female only) were appointed in the early church as servants of God's people. Their original purpose, as seen in Acts 6, seems to have been to care for those Christians who were in physical need, thus freeing the apostles to minister the Word and to devote themselves to prayer. The apostle Paul later points out that deacons and deaconesses must demonstrate high standards of morality, even as they carry out their practical and often low-profile deeds of service.

death. Viewed theologically, *death* refers to the destructive consequences of the entrance of sin into humankind. This consequence is spiritual alienation or separation from God. As a result of sin humans also experience physical death, a visible and universal reminder of the ongoing effects of sin. Scripture also points to a "second death" (Rev 2:11; 20:6, 14; 21:8): the final separation of the wicked from God's glorious presence for all eternity.

death of God movement. A theological movement popularized by Protestant theologians Thomas J. J. Altizer, William Hamilton and Paul van Buren in the 1960s, which declared that the traditional concept of God had ceased to play any significant role in the life of modern people. The movement was highly publicized by popular media but had a relatively short lifespan.

deconstruction. A term used primarily in *hermeneutics (the art and science of interpreting written texts or spoken language) to describe the process of analyzing a particular representation of reality so as to offer a critique of how a text "constructs" a picture of reality. Although deconstructionists are not always explicitly negative in practice, they often use deconstruction as a technique to discredit a text to which they are philosophically or ideologically opposed. Deconstruction, which is sometimes known as poststructuralism, arose out of, and in response to, a theory of literature called *structuralism, which sought to analyze the common structures that characterize various texts or literary works.

decree. Most simply, any command or order given by a human ruler for the sake of carrying out the task of governing or leading. From a theological perspective God's decrees are God's eternal, all-encompassing plans for creation. After the *Reformation certain *Calvinist theologians engaged in debates over the logical order of God's eternal decrees. The four decrees usually discussed included the decree to create, the decree to allow the *Fall into sin, the decree to *elect those who would receive *salvation and the decree to *damn the nonelect. *See also* sublapsarianism, infralapsarianism; supralapsarianism.

deification. In early non-Christian religions, the elevation of a human ruler to the status of deity. However, in *Eastern Orthodox theology *deification* is used to characterize *salvation, as suggested by 2 Peter 1:2-4. *Eastern Orthodoxy is careful to distinguish between the deification of the believer (as a "partaker" or "sharer" in the divine nature) and the deity of Christ (as actually being divine) as two qualitatively different categories.

deism. The belief that understands God as distant, in that God created the universe but then left it to run its course on its own, following certain "laws of nature" that God had built into the universe. An analogy often used to illustrate the deist view is that of an artisan who creates a mechanical clock, winds it up and then leaves the clock alone to "run out." Deism became popular in the early modern era and was prevalent among several of the founding fathers of the United States of America, including George Washington, Benjamin Franklin and Thomas Jefferson.

demon. Derived from the Greek terms *daimōn* and *daimonion*, demons are created spiritual beings who, along with Satan, are in rebellion against the good purposes of God. These "unclean spirits" seek to oppose, afflict and deceive Christians and non-Christians alike and to incite humans to rebel against God and God's good purposes for humankind and creation.

demythologizing. The term used by Rudolf *Bultmann to describe his approach to interpreting the Scriptures. Bultmann believed that the modern mind cannot accept the ancient worldview of the Bible, which included belief in demons, heaven, hell and miracles. Therefore, the task of interpretation is to identify the ancient "*myths" (symbols) found in the text and replace them with modern equivalents (which are also myths in Bultmann's definition). In this sense, Bultmann's demythologizing was not so much directed against myths themselves as against using outdated myths.

denomination, denominationalism. An organizational structure of several congregations who unite together on the basis of common doctrinal, organizational, ethnic, geographical or practical considerations even while meeting in separate localized situations. Denominationalism as a theory understands the church as consisting of a diversity of practices and beliefs under the umbrella of the larger term *Christian* while at the same time denying that any one Christian group can claim to be the exclusive manifestation of the church on earth. This is in contrast to *sectarianism (*see* sect, sectarianism) which refers to the attitude in which a narrowly defined group sees itself as the only true manifestation of the church to the exclusion of all other groups.

deposit of faith. The sum total of the teaching of the prophets and apostles about the way of *salvation through Jesus Christ, which has been written down in Scripture and is to be faithfully interpreted by the church and its teachers through the help of the Holy Spirit.

depravity, total depravity. *Depravity* refers both to the damaged relationship between God and humans and to the corruption of human nature such that there is within every human an ongoing tendency toward sin. *Total depravity* refers to the extent and comprehensiveness of the effects of sin on all humans such that all are unable to do anything to obtain *salvation. Total depravity, therefore, does not mean that humans are thoroughly sinful but rather that they are totally incapable of saving themselves. The term suggests as well that the effects of the *Fall extend to every dimension of human existence, so that we dare not trust any ability (such as reason) that we remain capable of exercising in our fallen state.

descent into hades (hell). The belief confessed in later versions of the Apostles' Creed that at some point between Christ's death and *resurrection, he visited the abode of those already dead (Greek *hadēs* or Hebrew *sheol*) either to proclaim the *salvation he had accomplished on the cross or, in some interpretations, to proclaim victory over Satan. Although there is some scriptural merit to the idea of Christ's descent into hades (Eph 4:9-10; 1 Pet 3:19-20) as a literal event, it has not been universally recognized in the church and instead has often been understood symbolically as representing the full extent of Christ's suffering on behalf of sinners—past, present and future.

determinism. Any theory that sees all events, including human behavior, as the necessary result of prior causes. Naturalistic determinism sees all events as part of an inflexible and unalterable chain of cause and effect in the physical universe. Theological determinism sees all events as being directly caused by God. Many theologians (although there are notable exceptions) reject both naturalistic and theological determinism because both theories seem to contradict the possibility of human freedom of choice, which in their view leaves humans morally not responsible for their actions.

deus absconditus, deus revelatus. Literally, "the hidden God" and "the revealed God," respectively. The phrases, originally used together by Martin Luther, speak of the paradoxical situation of a hidden God revealing himself and a revealed God hiding himself. For Luther the unknowable God is revealed in Christ; yet in the cross of Christ, God's true glory is hidden to human wisdom.

deus ex machina. Latin for "a god from a machine," the *deus ex machina* was a dramatic device used in ancient Greek and Roman drama whereby a "god" would be unexpectedly introduced into a play to provide a solution to an otherwise unsolvable problem. In the history of theology some theologians have been accused of introducing a "god of the gaps," or a *deus ex machina*, as a solution to a theological, philosophical or scientific problem where a more "rational" or "natural" solution may be possible. For example, some critics suggest that the Christian doctrine of God as Creator is a *deus ex machina* in that it posits God as the ultimate source of the universe rather than explaining the origin of the universe through a more "natural" or "scientific" theory. *See also* Occam's razor.

dialectical theology. A synonym for *neo-orthodoxy, dialectical theology is the general designation given to the theological contributions of several twentieth-century theologians, including Karl *Barth, Emil *Brunner and Rudolf *Bultmann. More specifically, *dialectical theology* refers to Karl Barth's focus on the qualitative difference between God and humans and the interplay (dialectic) between opposing or paradoxical ideas, such as time and eternity or finite and infinite.

dialogical personalism. The term used to refer to Martin Buber's attempt to distinguish between two types of relationships: the *I-Thou* relationship and the *I-It* relationship. The I-Thou relationship is characterized by mutuality between persons in ongoing conversation; in the I-It relationship a single person acts as the knowing subject and the *It* stands as the object to be known. For Buber true knowledge of God is a dialogical I-Thou relationship; that is, God is not an object to be studied but an active subject who comes into mutual and reciprocal relationship and conversation with humans.

diaspora. A Greek term originally meaning "the dispersed or scattered ones." The word was applied to individual Jews or communities of Jews who were scattered or mixed among the Gentile world. In NT usage the term is also used of Christians who were dispersed among the world, that is, in a context that is not their true "home" (see 1 Pet 1:1).

dichotomy, dichotomist. Literally, a dichotomy is a division of items into two mutually exclusive categories. Though there are several ways that dichotomy is used in theology (such as the distinction between God and humans, and between time and eternity), it often refers to the theory that humans are composed of two distinct components: body and soul. When applied to a theory of what constitutes reality (*metaphysics), theological dichotomists assert that reality is divided into two realms: the material (which is physical and concrete) and the immaterial (which is spiritual and abstract).

dispensationalism. A system of theology popularized mainly in twentieth-century North America, especially through the influence of the Scofield Reference Bible. The dispensationalism delineated by Scofield suggested that God works with humans in distinct ways (dispensations) through history; that God has a distinct plan for Israel over against the church; that the Bible, especially predictive prophecy, needs to be interpreted literally; that the church will be secretly *raptured from earth seven years prior to Christ's second coming; and that Christ will rule with Israel during a literal thousand-year earthly reign. Contemporary, or progressive, dispensationalism remains thoroughly *premillennial but rejects the *ontological distinction between Israel and the church as two peoples of God, seeing them instead as two salvation-historical embodiments of a single people.

docetism. In the early church, the teaching that Jesus was fully God but only *appeared* to be human (taken from the Greek *dokeō*, "to seem or appear"). Docetist theologians emphasized the qualitative difference between God and humans and therefore downplayed the human elements of Jesus' life in favor of those that pointed to his deity. The early church rejected docetism as an heretical interpretation of the biblical teaching about Jesus.

doctrine. A theological formulation that attempts to provide a summary statement of the teaching of Scripture on a particular theological topic. Ideally, doctrine is formed by attempting to be faithful to Scripture while giving attention to the traditions of the church and the thought patterns of the day. Thus doctrine is stated in such a way that contemporary people can understand the teaching of the ancient Scriptures.

documentary hypothesis. Also known as the JEDP theory, the documentary hypothesis arose out of the work of nineteenth-century OT scholars K. Graf and J. Wellhausen. They suggested that the Pentateuch (the first five books of the OT) was actually a compilation of the work of at least four separate sources, designated as the J (Jehovah) source, the E (Elohim) source, the D (Deuteronomist) source and the P (Priestly) source. The hypothesis stirred great controversy among conservative scholars who generally accepted Moses as the sole author of the Pentateuch.

dogma, dogmatics. In *Protestant circles *dogma is nearly synonymous to *doctrine, that is, a theological teaching. In Roman Catholic and *Eastern Orthodox circles dogmas are the officially accepted teaching of the church and not simply the theories of individual theologians. The term *dogmatics* generally refers to the churchly task of summarizing and systematizing the teaching of Scripture and tradition into a coherent whole according to the theological categories (such as *anthropology, *Christology, *soteriology) traditionally used throughout much of the history of the church.

dominical saying. Literally a "saying of the Lord" (*Lord* in Latin = *dominus*), it is a synonymous term in Gospel studies for a "saying of Jesus."

Donatism. During the fourth and fifth centuries A.D., a movement arising out of the initial teaching of Donatus sought to separate the "pure" church from the "apostate," or "fallen," church. The Donatists vigorously opposed Christian involvement in the military because the military was seen an instrument of the evil state. Donatists also urged that Christians be rebaptized if they had been baptized by a bishop who had cooperated with the pagan emperor. *Augustine eventually refuted the Donatist arguments.

dualism. Generally, any system of thought that attempts to define the nature of something as being composed of two distinct realities, substances or principles. In describing the nature of reality dualists usually posit a distinction between the physical and the spiritual (*see* Augustine) or between the invisible and the visible (*see* Plato). When describing the body, dualists (such as René Descartes) may distinguish between body and soul or between matter and mind. Other dualists may posit the existence of two opposing realities of good and evil (such as in *Gnosticism or *Manichaeanism).

Duns Scotus, Scotism (c. 1266-1308). A medieval Franciscan monk, philosopher and theologian who generally opposed the teaching of Thomas *Aquinas. Scotus argued that faith is more a matter of exercise of will than of reason. As a result, Scotism is the assertion that when the conclusions of philosophy (reason) come into conflict with the conclusions of theology (faith), the conclusions of faith must be accepted. Eventually the name *Duns* (dunce) became a term of ridicule, especially by certain Protestant Reformers, for those who believed without reason.

E

Eastern Orthodoxy. A branch of Christianity that is committed to preserving the doctrines formulated by the early church fathers as outlined in the seven ecumenical councils of the fourth through the eighth centuries. Although sharing certain theological commitments with Roman Catholicism and *Protestantism (such as the doctrine of the *Trinity), Eastern Orthodoxy is characterized by at least three major distinctives: (1) *apophatic theology, which suggests that because God is beyond rational understanding, a person can only know God as an "inner vision of light"; (2) the trinitarian understanding of the Spirit proceeding from the Father alone (as in the original wording of the *Nicene Creed) and not also from the Son (as in the Western version of the Creed); and (3) *salvation as a process of *deification, that is, of participating in the divine nature. *See also filioque.*

Ebionism. The teaching of an early group of Jewish-Christian sects that were committed to an *ascetic or poor lifestyle (from Hebrew *'ebonim,* "poor"). Ebionites rejected the Pauline epistles, concentrated on the theme of doing good works according to the book of James, saw the Christian life as strict obedience to a moral code and understood Jesus as one who was anointed by God at his baptism because of his perfect obedience to the Mosaic law. Although Ebionism was not officially condemned by the church, it never gained widespread acceptance.

ecclesiology. The area of theological study concerned with understanding the church (derived from the Greek word *ekklēsia,* "church"). Ecclesiology seeks to set forth the nature and function of the church. It also investigates issues such as the mission, ministry and structure of the church, as well as its role in the overall plan of God.

economic Trinity. Refers to the manifestations of the three persons of the *Trinity in relationship to the world, particularly in regard to the outworking of God's plan (economy) of *salvation. Thus the economic Trinity refers to how God as a tripersonal being relates to the world, which in turn provides the biblical context for understanding how the persons of the Trinity relate to each other (*immanent Trinity). One of the most important contemporary theological questions surrounding the Trinity asks: Is there a difference between "God in relationship to the world" (economic Trinity) and "God in internal eternal relationship" (immanent Trinity)?

ecumenism, ecumenical movement. From the Greek word *oikoumenē,* "the entire inhabited earth." Ecumenism is the attempt to seek a worldwide unity and cooperation among all churches that confess Jesus Christ as Lord. Ecumenism recognizes the unfortunate effect of many schisms in church history, the most major being the division between Eastern and Western churches in 1054 and between Protestants and Roman Catholics during the *Reformation in the sixteenth century. In the early twentieth century various international missionary conferences explored the need for Christian unity if world evangelization were to be accomplished. This gave birth to the modern ecumenical movement. Positively, the ecumenical movement reaffirmed the need for all branches of Christianity to see their common roots and to seek unity where possible. Negatively, the ecumenical movement has often focused on political ideology; consequently, sectors of the Christian church have been hesitant to join in ecumenical dialog.

Edwards, Jonathan (1703-1758). One of the greatest American theologians and pastors, Edwards ministered as a Massachusetts Congregational pastor and was intimately involved with the first Great Awakening. Edwards is recognized for his efforts to give a theological explanation of that movement and for giving shape to *Calvinism in eighteenth-century North America.

efficacy, efficacious. A term that describes the ability of something to fulfill the purpose for which it is made or given. The term usually is used in reference to the purposes and grace of God. God's grace, then, is efficacious inasmuch as it is able to bring about *salvation in those to whom it is directed. Thus efficacious grace is the only grace capable of completely bringing about the salvation of the human being and can be offered only by God.

election. A biblical word used to speak of God's choosing of individuals or people to bring about God's good purposes. In general terms *election* can refer to God's choosing of persons for a type of service, while in a more particular sense *election* refers to God's choosing of persons to inherit *salvation through Jesus Christ. The doctrine of election has been the subject of intense debate, particularly between *Calvinist and *Arminian theologians, since the *Reformation era. Other theologians (e.g., Karl *Barth) try to avoid the Calvinist-Arminian debate by suggesting that God's election is first and foremost an election of Christ rather than the election of individuals to salvation.

elements. Refers to the physical symbols used in the *ordinances or *sacraments of the church, especially the *Lord's Supper. Hence the bread and the wine are the "elements" of the Lord's Supper, or *Eucharist. In particular, theologians over the centuries have debated whether Christ is in some way present in the elements, and if so, in what way—physically or spiritually? This debate arises particularly out of an examination of Christ's own words at the Last Supper, "This [bread] is my body" (Lk 22:19; see 1 Cor 11:24). *See also* consubstantiation; transubstantiation.

emanation. A term meaning literally "a flowing down from." The term arose out of ancient Greek philosophies that understood creation to be an overflow of the fullness of God rather than something created by God out of nothing *(ex nihilo)*. The idea of creation as an emanation of God was used by certain medieval philosophers and theologians to suggest that creation is really a hierarchy of order flowing down from God through the spiritual world of angels, the material world of humans and animals, and finally to the world of physical objects. *See also creatio ex nihilo.*

empiricism. A philosophical theory that assumes that all knowledge is gained through either internal experience (thoughts, emotions, etc.) or external experience (sight, smell, touch, hearing and taste). Empiricism is most closely associated with individuals such as Francis Bacon and John Locke, but the purest form of empiricism is found in the thought of David Hume. Hume took empiricism to its extreme, stating that a person can not really know if external things (objects) exist because all one can know for certain is one's own experience of those things.

Enlightenment, the. A term used to refer primarily to the philosophical mood among seventeenth- and eighteenth-century Western intellectuals. During the eighteenth century the philosopher Immanuel *Kant defined the Enlightenment as "mankind's coming of age." Enlightenment thinkers rejected external authorities as a source of knowledge and instead elevated human reasoning as the best way to bring about an understanding of the world. As a result, the Enlightenment era brought with it a suspicion of the claims to authority of the Bible, the church, the *creeds and any religious *dogmas or doctrines.

episcopacy, episcopal. A form of church government in which the chief oversight of the church is entrusted to bishops, while presbyters, *deacons or priests minister more specifically within local congregations. Episcopal government is hierarchical, with a college of bishops or a head bishop exercising highest authority. Roman Catholic, *Eastern Orthodox and *Anglican churches represent major forms of episcopacy. The head bishop of the Roman Catholic Church is the pope of Rome; of the Eastern Orthodox Church, the patriarchate of Constantinople; and of the Anglican Church, the group of bishops headed by the archbishop of Canterbury.

epistemology. Philosophical inquiry into the nature, sources, limits and methods of gaining knowledge. In Western philosophy, epistemology has generally followed two main alternatives: rationalism (knowledge is gained through the mind's use of reason and logic) and *empiricism (knowledge is gained through the gathering of information through the use of the inner and external senses).

equivocal. In semantics (the study of the meanings of words) the term is used to identify words that have more than one possible meaning. This is in contrast to *univocal words, which have only one possible meaning. In theology a term is said to be equivocal if it means something quite different when used of God than when referring to humans or something else in creation.

Erasmus, Desiderius (c. 1466-1536). A major figure of the Reformation period, Erasmus, a Christian *humanist, sought to bring about reforms in the church through a return to scholarly study of both the Scriptures and the texts of the Greek and Latin and Latin classical tradition. One of Erasmus's major undertakings was the production of a Greek New Testament. Erasmus is significant in that he provided the tools that Reformers such as Luther and Calvin used in their efforts to interpret the NT on the basis of the Greek text and to carry on their theological work.

eschaton, eschatology (consistent [thoroughgoing], realized, inaugurated). Derived from the Greek term meaning "last," *eschaton* refers to the ultimate climax or end of history wherein Christ returns to earth to establish his eternal kingdom of righteousness and justice among all nations. Eschatology, then, is the theological study that seeks to understand the ultimate direction or purpose of history as it moves toward the future, both from an individual perspective (What happens when a person dies?) and from a corporate perspective (Where is history going, and how will it end?). In the twentieth century at least three basic forms of eschatology have developed. Consistent, or thoroughgoing, eschatology is the view that the teaching of Jesus and the apostles is thoroughly concerned with proclaiming the imminent end of history. Realized eschatology views the first coming of Jesus Christ itself as the full presence of the kingdom of God. Inaugurated eschatology sees the first coming of Christ as the beginning of the kingdom in the present, while acknowledging that the consummation or fulfillment of the kingdom of God is yet to come.

essence, *essentia*. Deriving from the Latin verb *esse,* literally "to be," essence is the fundamental nature of something apart from which the thing would not be what it is. Essence, then, is the core of what makes something what it is without being something else. The Latin term *essentia* became important in reference to the nature of God, especially in the discussion surrounding the *Trinity, where each person—Father, Son and Holy Spirit—is said to share the same *essentia*.

eternal generation of the Son. A phrase used to describe the relationship that exists between the first and second persons of the *Trinity. God the Father is said to generate (or "beget") the Son eternally. In other words, the Son's identity as Son is defined eternally by his relationship to the Father. Likewise, the Father is eternally the Father by his relationship to the Son. The "generation" of the Son is not to be confused with physical conception or birth, whereby a human father begets a son who did not previously exist. In other words, the eternal generation of the Son does not speak about the origin of the Son but rather seeks to define the relationship of the Son to the Father.

eternity, eternality. In the absolute sense, eternity is the realm in which there is no beginning and no end. As a term relative to the concept of time, *eternity* is what lies beyond time and is not constrained by time. Eternality, then, is the characteristic or attribute associated with God alone, because God has no beginning point and no ending point. Eternality applies only to God in another way as well: only God is uncaused.

ethics. The area of philosophical and theological inquiry into what constitutes right and wrong, that is, morality, as well as what is the good and the good life. Ethics seeks to provide insight, principles or even a system of guidance in the quest of the good life or in acting rightly in either general or specific situations of life. Broadly speaking, ethical systems are either deontological (seeking to guide behavior through establishment or discovery of what is intrinsically right and wrong) or *teleological (seeking to guide behavior through an understanding of the outcomes or ends that ethical decisions and behavior bring about).

Eucharist. From the Greek word *eucharistō* (I give thanks), the term has been used in the Christian tradition to refer to one of the central rites of the church, namely, the ongoing commemoration of the last supper that Christ had with his disciples before his crucifixion or the commemoration of the crucifixion itself. As such, the Eucharist is a celebration of thanksgiving to God for the redemptive work of Christ. The term *Eucharist* (or *Mass*) has generally been used in Roman Catholic and Anglican traditions, while Protestant traditions generally prefer to speak of the celebration as the Lord's *Supper, *Communion or "the breaking of bread."

evangelical, evangelicalism, neo-evangelicalism. A set of terms arising out of the Greek word *euangelion,* "good news," or "gospel." In its most general sense *evangelical* means being characterized by a concern for the essential core of the Christian message, which proclaims the possibility of *salvation through the person and work of Jesus Christ. More specifically, *evangelicalism* has been used to refer to the transdenominational and international movement that emphasizes the need to experience personal *conversion through belief in Christ and his work on the cross, and a commitment to the authority of Scripture as the infallible guide for Christian faith and practice. *Neo-evangelicalism* is the classification given particularly to a movement of North American Christians that arose initially in the 1940s. Neo-evangelicals were initially interested in proclaiming not only the personal but also the social dimensions of the gospel, such as the need to work for justice for those who are socially oppressed as well as to offer care and relief to those who suffer physically.

evidentialism. A method of defending the Christian faith (*apologetics) that assumes that data drawn from history and experience (facts) can demonstrate the reasonableness of Christian claims and can therefore help to prepare a person for faith in Christ by removing obstacles to belief. Thus evidentialism attempts to give as much "evidence" as possible to substantiate crucial facts of the Christian faith such as the resurrection of Christ or the historical accuracy of the biblical accounts.

evil. Any act or event that is contrary to the good and holy purposes of God. Theologians generally distinguish between *moral* and *natural* evil. Moral evil refers to acts (sins) of creatures that are contrary to God's holy character and law. Natural evils include harmful or destructive events in nature that occur throughout the course of history and that negatively affect creaturely life (e.g., earthquakes and famines). Some theologians (e.g., *Augustine) emphasize that evil does not have independent existence as a "thing" but is either the moral evaluation of acts or the ultimate consequence or effect of such evil acts on creation.

ex opere operato, ex opere operantis. Two Latin phrases employed particularly in reference to the debate over the effectiveness of the *sacraments. *Ex opere operato* literally means "from the work done" and suggests that a sacrament is effective in fulfilling its purpose. This effectiveness is not dependent on the faith of the recipient of the grace that comes through the act. In addition, the concept may suggest that the sacrament is effective even if it is administered by a sinful person or perhaps even by a person who is not properly *ordained by the church. *Ex opere operantis* literally means "from the work of the one doing the work" and suggests that the sacrament is effective only if administered rightly by a duly ordained priest or minister of the church.

exclusivism. Any theory that argues that *salvation is found only in and through Jesus Christ to the exclusion of all other religions or beliefs. Exclusivism also generally argues that Christ must be believed upon and explicitly *confessed in order for a person to qualify for salvation. As a consequence, exclusivists tend to reject the possibility of salvation for those who have never heard the gospel of Jesus Christ. *See also* inclusivism.

exegesis, eisegesis. Literally, "drawing meaning out of" and "reading meaning into," respectively. Exegesis is the process of seeking to understand what a text means or communicates on its own. *Eisegesis* is generally a derogatory term used to designate the practice of imposing a preconceived or foreign meaning onto a text, even if that meaning could not have been originally intended at the time of its writing.

exemplarism. The belief that Jesus' life and ministry is primarily an example to humans of how to live uprightly before God rather than a means of providing something that humans cannot gain on their own. Many opponents of exemplarism argue that the theory assumes that humans in their sinful condition have the ability to conform to the character and life of Jesus.

existentialism. Any philosophical system that attempts to define what it means to be human in terms of "existence" (How does a human live?) rather than in terms of "*essence" (What is a human?) Existentialists generally agree that there is no essence common to humankind but that persons are all uniquely defined by their free decisions and acts. As a result, existentialists tend to elevate personal freedom and emphasize the need to "make" life meaningful rather than seeking to "find" the meaning of life.

expiation. The belief that sin is canceled out by being covered over. For Christians, expiation suggests that Christ's death covers our sins. Biblical scholars debate whether the Greek terms deriving from *hilaskomai* should be translated as "*propitiation*," denoting the turning away of divine wrath, or, in contrast, as "expiation," denoting the sense of covering sins or canceling a debt. *Hilaskomai* is also sometimes translated simply as "mercy seat."

extra nos. Literally, "outside of ourselves." The Latin term is often used in reference to the location or source of *salvation as being completely external to the human being. In other words, to suggest that salvation is *extra nos* is to deny that salvation occurs on the basis of anything inherent in humans, whether a human act of the will or a human thought. Instead, salvation *extra nos* affirms that salvation is completely an act of God; that is, God freely and sovereignly bestows salvation upon a person.

F

faith. A biblical word that refers both to intellectual belief and to relational trust or commitment. The biblical authors generally do not make a distinction between faith as belief and faith as trust, but tend to see true faith as consisting of both what is believed (e.g., that God exists, that Jesus is Lord) and the personal commitment to a person who is trustworthy, reliable and able to save (that is, trust in the person of Christ as the way to *salvation). *See also* assensus; fiducia; notitia.

Fall. The event in which Adam and Eve, the first humans, disobeyed the explicit command of God, thereby bringing sin and death onto the human race. As a consequence of the Fall humans have become alienated from God, from one another and from the created order.

federal theology, federal headship. A theological system of thought identified with the work of Johannes Cocceius (1603-1669) and often called *covenant theology. Federal theology suggests that as the first human, Adam acted as the "federal head" (from Latin *foedus,* "covenant") or legal representative of the rest of humankind. Thus God entered into a covenantal relationship with Adam that promised blessing for obedience and a curse for disobedience. According to federal theology, if Adam had been obedient to God, his obedience would have meant blessing for all humans. But because Adam was disobedient, the curse extends to humankind, of which Adam is the covenantal representative. Federal theology adds that just as Adam was the federal head of humanity, so also Christ enters history as a second Adam, free from the curse, and acts as the covenantal head of righteousness for all those who believe in him.

feminism. Any movement that attempts to emphasize or recover female perspectives on reality and the world. In theology and biblical studies, feminism in its broadest sense has sought to show both God's feminine characteristics and how Scripture has often been interpreted with male biases and assumptions. In its most radical forms, theological feminism argues that God should be addressed with feminine titles (such as Goddess or Mother) and that many parts of the Bible, especially the OT, are at best patriarchal (and thus irrelevant) or at worst antiwoman (and thus oppressive to women). In more moderate forms, feminism seeks to provide feminine language and perspectives in theological reflection on God, while not abandoning the traditional titles of Father, Son and Spirit in reference to the *Trinity.

fideism. The view that matters of religious and theological truth must be accepted by faith apart from the exercise of reason. In its extreme, fideism suggests that the use of reason is misleading. Less extreme fideists suggest that reason is not so much misleading as it is simply unable to lead to truths about the nature of God and *salvation.

fides qua creditur, fides quae creditur. Literally, "the faith by which (it) is believed" and "the faith which is believed," respectively. The terms refer to two aspects of Christian faith: the internal and the external. The *fides qua creditur* is the means by which God's self-revelation is received (that is, the exercise of trust in God as an internal attitude), while *fides quae creditur* is the actual content or composition of what is revealed by God (that is, the intellectual acceptance of certain statements about God). *Fides qua creditur* speaks to the question of *how* one believes in God; *fides quae creditur* speaks to the question of *what* one believes about God.

fides quaerens intellectum. Literally, "faith seeking understanding." The phrase originated with *Anselm in his *Proslogion* and was used to show the relationship of religious faith to human reason. For Anselm, matters of religion and theology are understood only by first believing them and then proceeding to gain an intellectual understanding of the things already believed. In other words, faith is both logically and chronologically prior to reason.

fiducia. Literally, "trust." In Latin *fiducia* refers to the essential nature of faith (Latin, *fides*); that is, to exercise *faith is to engage in trust or commitment. Although related, *fiducia* is distinguished from * *assensus,* which refers to intellectual acceptance of certain propositions or truths. Biblical faith affirms the importance of both *fiducia* and *assensus. See also* notitia.

filioque. A Latin term literally meaning "and the Son," *filioque* became significant because of its addition to the description of the Holy Spirit in the Niceno-Constantinopolitan *Creed (A.D. 381) by the Western (Latin) churches in the sixth century. Originally the Creed stated that the Holy Spirit proceeds from the Father, but the addition of *filioque* suggested that the Holy Spirit proceeds from both the Father "and the Son." The addition of the *filioque* clause without the consensus of the Eastern churches ignited a great controversy and became a major factor in the subsequent split between the Eastern and Western churches in A.D. 1054.

Five Ways, the. The five rational arguments that Thomas *Aquinas saw as pointing to the existence of God. The five arguments are (1) the argument from *motion* (all things in motion need a mover, but there must be something unmoved that begins other things in motion; God is this Unmoved Mover); (2) the * *cosmological* argument (all effects must have causes, but there cannot be an infinite series of causes into the past; thus God is the first or Uncaused Cause); (3) the argument from * *contingency* (all things exist in dependence on something else, that is, contingent; therefore there must be something that is absolutely independent, that is, necessary; this necessary being is God); (4) the argument from *perfection* (there appears to be an increasing degree of perfection among things; therefore there must be a being who is the height of perfection; this Being is God); and (5) the *teleological* argument (the observable design in the world suggests that there must be an intelligent designer—God).

foreknowledge. A biblical term (from Greek *prognōsis*) that literally means "to know in advance." Some theologians view foreknowledge as referring to God's selective choice of individuals or groups of people with whom to enter into a loving relationship. Foreknowledge understood in this sense is more than simply knowing events in advance of their happening (although this may be included) because the Scriptures seem to use the term in a more relational than chronological sense. Thus the foreknowledge of God involves God's favorable disposition to certain people, even before they existed.

foundationalism. A term referring to any theory of knowledge that looks for a starting point or "foundation" on which to build knowledge. This foundation may take the form of an indisputable proposition or set of propositions on which knowledge can be constructed through the use of logical reasoning from the first propositions. Historically, René Descartes is credited with being one of the greatest foundationalist philosophers. Descartes begins his whole system of knowledge by affirming the now-famous dictum *cogito ergo sum* (I think, therefore I am). Alternatively, some foundationalists (e.g., Friedrich *Schleiermacher) have sought to construct knowledge on the basis of some supposedly universal human experience.

free churches, free church movement. Terms used to designate those churches or *denominations that have deliberately separated themselves from the influence, support or control of the state or government. The free church movement arose primarily as a reaction to the Roman Catholicism of the Middle Ages and later to the *Calvinist and Lutheran churches, which maintained a close connection with the state.

free will. The belief that human behavior is self-caused. The idea of free will assumes that there are no external causes sufficient to explain why a person acts as he or she does. Actions, according to free-will theory, are ultimately chosen, even if the person choosing knows that the chosen action may bring about undesirable consequences.

free will theism. A late-twentieth-century theological development in the doctrine of God that seeks to steer a middle path between a "classical" view of God as largely unaffected by human creatures and a "process" view that understands God to be integrally involved and constantly changing with creation. Instead free will theism asserts that God enters into a "give-and-take" relationship with humanity and freely risks his sovereignty by giving humans a substantial measure of freedom. Arguably the main thinker behind the "free will theism" idea is the Canadian theologian Clark H. Pinnock. *See also* process theology.

fundamentalism, fundamentalist-modernist debate. A movement in North America during the early part of the twentieth century that attempted to maintain a firm commitment to certain "fundamentals" of the Christian faith. Fundamentalism was a direct reaction to the increasing influence of "*liberal" or "*modernist" forms of Christianity that were becoming increasingly popular within American Protestant seminaries and churches. The fundamentalist-modernist debate pitted modernists, who tended to reject the supernatural elements of the biblical witness, against fundamentalists, who emphasized the historicity of the miraculous events recorded in Scripture, including the *virgin birth and the *resurrection, as well as belief in the second coming of Christ.

G

general revelation. A term used to declare that God reveals something about the divine nature through the created order. This self-revealing of God through creation is called general because it only gives "general" or "indirect" information about

God, including the fact of God's existence and that God is powerful. This is in contrast to special revelation, which is more "specific" and "direct," and includes the appearance of the living Word (Jesus Christ himself) and the written Word of God (the Scriptures), revealing a holy, loving and just God who graciously provides forgiveness of sin. General revelation is likewise "general" in that it is available to all humankind, in contrast to the divine self-disclosure that God revealed to certain persons. *See also* special revelation.

genre. A term that refers to different types or varieties of literature or media. In the interpretation of texts, particularly the Bible, most exegetes agree that identifying the genre of the text to be interpreted is crucial and that the text must be understood in light of the common conventions that typified that genre at the time of its writing. Thus, poetry is not to be interpreted in the same manner as historical narrative, nor is prophecy properly read in the same manner as an epistle (letter).

glorification. The last stage in the process of *salvation, namely, the *resurrection of the body at the second coming of Jesus Christ and the entrance into the eternal *kingdom of God. In glorification believers attain complete conformity to the image and likeness of the glorified Christ and are freed from both physical and spiritual defect. Glorification ensures that believers will never again experience bodily decay, death or illness, and will never again struggle with sin.

glory. A biblical term used in reference to the unapproachable and mighty manifestation of the immediate presence of God. The biblical concept of glory carries with it connotations of inexpressible beauty and majesty. At the same time it implies an absolutely pure and terrifying "holiness" confronting the sinfulness of humans. In the NT, Christ is said to be the glory of God, although a glory that is at least partially veiled from sight, except for those who exercise faith in Christ. Christ's glory is especially a consequence of his *resurrection from the dead and his *ascension to the right hand of the Father.

glossolalia. A compound Greek word meaning "to speak in tongues" (from *laleō,* "to speak" and *glōssa,* "tongue"). Glossolalia, the supernatural ability to speak in languages not previously learned, is first recorded in Scripture as happening on the day of Pentecost (Acts 2). The apostle Paul later makes reference to glossolalia as a special gift of the Spirit given to some Christians and to be practiced for the edification of the church. Throughout church history there has been ongoing debate as to whether genuine glossolalia ceased after the passing of the apostles or if it is a legitimate gift to be practiced today.

Gnosticism. An early Greek religious movement of broad proportions that was particularly influential in the second-century church. Many biblical interpreters see in certain NT documents (such as 1 John) the attempt to answer or refute Gnostic teaching. The word *gnosticism* comes from the Greek term *gnosis*, meaning "knowledge." Gnostics believed that devotees had gained a special kind of spiritual enlightenment, through which they had attained a secret or higher level of knowledge not accessible to the uninitiated. Gnostics also tended to emphasize the spiritual realm over the material, often claiming that the material realm is evil and hence to be escaped.

grace (common, efficacious, prevenient). One of the central concepts of the Scriptures, grace speaks of God's loving actions toward creation and toward humankind in particular. Grace is the generous overflow of the love of God the Father toward the Son, Jesus Christ. This love is most clearly demonstrated to humans through God's selfless giving of Jesus to enable people to enter into a loving relationship with God as the Holy Spirit enables them. *Common grace* speaks of God's extension of favor to all people through providential care, regardless of whether or not they acknowledge and love God. **Efficacious grace* refers to the special application of grace to a person who comes by faith to Christ for *salvation. It is the special act of God that brings about the true salvation of a person. **Prevenient grace*, though often thought to be synonymous with common grace, refers more specifically to the Wesleyan idea that God has enabled all people everywhere to respond favorably to the gospel if they so choose.

Gregory of Nazianzus (c. A.D. 329-389), Gregory of Nyssa (c. A.D. 335-395). Two early church theologians who together with *Basil the Great are known as the *Cappadocian fathers. Both were influential in the development of the orthodox statement of the doctrine of the *Trinity. Gregory of Nazianzus was significant in identifying distinctive terms to describe each of the persons of the Godhead: the Father is unbegotten, the Son is eternally begotten and the Spirit proceeds. Gregory of Nyssa contributed to trinitarian doctrine by working through the details of Basil's distinction between the one *ousia* ("substance" or "*essence") of God and the three trinitarian *hypostaseis* ("persons") of God.

H

hamartology. The term used to refer to the theological investigation of sin (from Greek *hamartia*, "sin"). Hamartology concerns itself with understanding the origin, nature, extent and consequences of sin. Furthermore, hamartology seeks to understand how sin is transmitted throughout the human race and how sin opposes God's purposes for creation.

Harnack, Adolf von (1851-1930). A German theologian and church historian whose major contributions were in NT studies and patristics (the study of the thought and writings of the early church Fathers). One of Harnack's central arguments was that the development of doctrine, or *dogma, in the early church led away from the original teachings of Jesus and his disciples. Harnack argued, therefore, that the task of the theologian and church historian is to strip away the "husk" of cultural and historical developments of doctrine and get back to the original "kernel" of the gospel found in Jesus. For Harnack, this kernel was Jesus' announcement of the *kingdom of God. This kingdom is based in the Fatherhood of God and the kinship of humankind, and it is fulfilled by Christians through the exercise of higher righteousness (love).

Hegel, Georg Wilhelm Friedrich (1770-1831). German philosopher and theologian who argued that "mind" or "spirit" (German *Geist*) is the only thing that is ultimately real and that everything else is a byproduct of "mind." Creation, then, is essentially the product of the divine mind. As a result, Hegel argued, to know how history unfolds is to understand the workings of the divine mind. Contradictions in history, whether contradictions of logic or contradictions involved in two nations standing in opposition to one another in war, always lead to a higher understanding or synthesis that transcends both sides.

Heidelberg Catechism. A confession of faith written by the theology faculty of Heidelberg University at the request of Frederick III, a prince of Germany in the sixteenth century. The Catechism served to instruct young people in the essentials of the faith and was used to prepare them for *confirmation. One unique feature of the Catechism is its ability to combine Reformed and Lutheran perspectives into a single document.

Heilsgeschichte **(salvation history).** A German term meaning "history of salvation." Originally coined by Johann Albrecht Bengel (1687-1752), the term was used to describe the nature of the Bible as an account of God's working out divine *salvation in human history. Proponents of this approach rejected the idea that the Bible is a collection of divine "proof texts" for constructing doctrine in favor of seeing it as the history of God's redemptive plan. In the middle of the twentieth century many theologians adopted elements of the *Heilsgeschichte* approach to biblical interpretation (e.g., Oscar Cullmann, Gerhard von Rad), although there were some notable exceptions (e.g., Rudolf *Bultmann).

heresy. Any teaching rejected by the Christian community as contrary to Scripture and hence to *orthodox doctrine. Most of the teachings that have been declared heretical have to do with either the nature of God or the person of Jesus Christ. The term *heresy* is not generally used to characterize non-Christian belief. That is to say, systems of belief such as *atheism or *agnosticism, or non-Christian religions such as Buddhism or Islam are not technically heresy. The term *heresy* is generally reserved for any belief that claims to be Christian and scriptural but has been rejected by the church as sub-Christian or antiscriptural.

hermeneutic of suspicion. A phrase first used by the French philosopher Paul Ricoeur to refer to the interpretative practice of coming to a text with questions or "suspicions" about its truthfulness or veracity. Conversely, a hermeneutic of suspicion allows the text to call into question the *reader's* assumptions and worldview.

hermeneutics. The discipline that studies the principles and theories of how texts ought to be interpreted, particularly sacred texts such as the Scriptures. Hermeneutics also concerns itself with understanding the unique roles and relationships between the author, the text and the original or subsequent readers.

historical criticism. An approach to biblical interpretation that seeks to understand the Bible in light of its historical and cultural backgrounds, that is, as a book arising out of a human context. Historical criticism uses a variety of methods to determine what actually happened in history "before," "behind" or "under" the text rather than seeking a "divine" meaning in the text itself. Although helpful to an extent, the primary criticism leveled against historical criticism is that it tends to downplay Scripture as a divine book and instead overemphasizes its humanness.

historical Jesus. A reference to the person of Jesus as he can be understood and investigated using the tools and methods of modern approaches to the study of history. The "historical Jesus" is often contrasted with "the Christ of faith," that is, the Jesus that is honored and preached about by the Christian church. In using these terms, it is often assumed that there is a gap between what can really be known about the historical person, that is, Jesus as he actually existed, and the Jesus proclaimed by the apostles as recorded in the NT documents.

historical theology. The division of the theological discipline that seeks to understand and delineate how the church interpreted Scripture and developed doctrine throughout its history, from the time of the apostles to the present day. The twofold function of historical theology is to show the origin and development of beliefs held in the present day and to help contemporary theologians identify theological errors of the past that should be avoided in the present.

historicism. A term used to describe one of two types of theories of history. In the first type, historicism is the theory that all things can be best understood as the result of historical development; that is, a thing is what it is because of its history. In the second type, historicism is the belief that history progresses through unstoppable forces and that historians can predict future historical outcomes on the basis of observed patterns in the past.

Holiness Movement. A movement among certain Protestant churches during the mid-1800s following in the tradition of John *Wesley. These churches emphasized Wesley's doctrine of "entire *sanctification," that is, that a Christian's life of purity takes place in two stages: through initial sanctification at *conversion and through a second event of sanctification later in the Christian's life (often called "the second blessing" or "entire sanctification") during which the Christian is freed from the bonds of the sinful nature, even though the believer continues to live in an imperfect body and an imperfect world.

holy. A biblical term generally meaning "to be set apart." The term is used widely in Scripture to refer to a variety of people and objects alike but ultimately points to God as the one who is qualitatively different or set apart from creation. *Holy* may also be used to describe someone or something that God has "set apart" for special purposes. In the NT holiness takes on the sense of ethical purity or freedom from sin. The fullness of the biblical witness, then, testifies to God's holiness, understood as God's "otherness" and "purity," as well as to God's prerogative to set people and things apart for God's own purposes, together with the resulting godliness in the lives of those whom God declares to be holy.

homiletics. The theological discipline that seeks to understand the purpose and process of preparing and delivering sermons. Homiletics seeks to integrate an understanding of the place of the preacher, the sermon and the audience. Homiletics also seeks to help preachers to prepare themselves spiritually for preaching, to develop sermons that are faithful to Scripture and to present the sermon in culturally relevant ways.

homoiousios, homoousios. Two Greek terms used in the third and fourth centuries in the debate surrounding the relationship of Jesus the Son to God the Father. *Homoiousios* (literally, "of similar substance") was used by Semi-Arians to argue that the Son was of similar but not identical substance as God the Father. *Homoousios* (literally, "same in substance") was used by *Athanasius and others to argue that the Son derives his substance from the Father and hence shares the same substance as the Father. *Homoousios* eventually became accepted as *orthodox teaching.

hope. A biblical term (Greek *elpis*) referring to the expectation of the believer that God will fulfill promises made in the past. Biblical hope is more than a simple wish; it entails certainty based on God's demonstration of faithfulness to people in the history of *salvation as recorded in the Scriptures and as experienced by the church. Ultimately the Christian's future hope lies in the promise of Christ's return and the anticipation of *resurrection from the dead. *See also* blessed hope.

humanism (secular humanism). In general, humanism is any movement or ideology that focuses on the worth of the human being. Christian humanism emphasizes the fact that humans are created in God's image and as such are creatures of worth or value. *Secular* humanism, on the other hand, attempts to see the worth of humans apart from any appeal to God. Thus humanists often suggest that value is completely intrinsic to the individual.

humiliation of Christ. A phrase used to speak of Jesus' voluntary giving up of his *glory as the Son of the Father in being born as a human, suffering and dying for the sake of humankind. Theologians have debated as to whether Christ's humiliation includes a descent into hell after his death, but most are in agreement that Jesus' life and death serve as the ultimate example of self-sacrifice for the sake of others.

hypostasis, hypostatic union. *Hypostasis* is a Greek noun first used by Eastern theologians in the early centuries of church history to refer to the three persons of the *Trinity. The *Cappadocian fathers, *Basil in particular, argued that God is three *hypostaseis* in one *ousia* ("*essence," or "substance"). Although helpful, the term also led to confusion. Western theologians described God as one *substantia* in three *personae*, with confusion arising out of the fact that *substantia* was the Latin equivalent to *hypostasis*. Technically, *hypostasis* refers to each of the three concrete and distinct trinitarian persons who share a single divine nature or essence. The hypostatic union, in contrast, is an important christological designation. At the *Council of Chalcedon in A.D.451 the church declared the doctrine of the hypostatic union. The doctrine is an attempt to describe the miraculous bringing together of humanity and divinity in the same person, Jesus Christ, such that he is both fully divine and fully human.

I

iconoclasm. Literally, "destruction of images." Historically, iconoclasm arose in the eighth century as the practice of destroying images (icons) of Jesus Christ often found in the gathering places of certain Christian churches. Many Christians worshiped the icons as representations of Jesus Christ in his physical incarnation. The iconoclastic controversy began in A.D. 725 when Emperor Leo III decided to have icons destroyed because he thought icon worship was idolatrous and a hindrance to the conversion of Jews and Muslims.

idealism. Any philosophical system that describes the nature of reality more in terms of spirit or mind than matter or material. Some idealists argue that all reality is the product of a single mind (or *Geist*), namely, the mind of God (*Hegelian idealism), while others suggest that reality is the sum total of many minds (Berkeleian idealism). Still others see reality as a hierarchy and deem the abstract realm of thoughts and ideas to be "more real" than the "less real" concrete realm of physical objects and shadows of objects (*Platonic idealism).

illumination. The ongoing work of the Holy Spirit in the Christian person and community in assisting believers to interpret, understand and obey the Scriptures. Illumination is a matter of faith as well as intellectual assent—the Spirit's goal in illumination moves beyond mere intellectual assent to propositions of Scripture to the moving of the human will to trust Christ and obey him.

imago Dei (image of God). A term describing the uniqueness of humans as God's creatures. In the Genesis creation account Adam and Eve are said to be created in God's image and likeness (Gen 1:26-27). Theologians differ on what the image of God actually refers to, but most agree that the image is not primarily physical. Instead the *imago Dei* may include the presence of will, emotions and reason; the ability to think and act creatively; or the ability to interact socially with others. Scripture attributes the *imago Dei* solely to humans, and it indicates that the image is in some sense still present even after the *Fall (see Jas 3:9). Above all, however, Christ—and by extension those who are in Christ— is the image of God.

immaculate conception. The Roman Catholic teaching that Mary the mother of Jesus was supernaturally prevented from being tainted by original sin so that she could give birth to Jesus as God's own Son. The teaching was first suggested by the theologian *Duns Scotus in the thirteenth century and declared to be official Roman Catholic *dogma (authoritative teaching) by Pope Pius IX in 1854.

immanence. The idea that God is present in, close to and involved with creation. Unlike *pantheism, which teaches that God and the world are one or that God is the "soul" (animating principle) of the world, Christian theology teaches that God is constantly involved with creation without actually becoming exhausted by creation or ceasing to be divine in any way. *See also* transcendence.

immanent Trinity. The term used to explore and, to an inadequate degree, explain the internal workings and relationships among the three persons of the *Trinity. Statements about the immanent Trinity seek to give language to the inexpressible mystery of what God is like apart from reference to God's dealings with creation. Thus the immanent Trinity is God-as-God-is throughout eternity. The Scriptures suggest that Jesus and the Father are one (Jn 10:30) and that the Holy Spirit is the Spirit of God and of Christ (1 Cor 2:10; 3:17-18). The Scriptures also suggest that love is the *essence of the immanent Trinity (see Jn 17:23-26; 1 Jn 4:8, 16). *See also* economic trinity.

imminence. A term usually referring to the possibility of Christ's second coming occurring at any moment. The imminence of Christ's return suggests that no established intervening events need to take place before his return, thus ruling out all predictions that would set the time or date of his coming. Some contemporary theologians reinterpret *imminence* to mean that Christ's return is near in the sense that it is the next major event in God's timetable for history.

immortality. Most simply, the inability to cease to exist or the ability to exist eternally. In this sense God is the only being who is truly immortal, because God has always existed and will not cease to exist. Some theologians argue, however, that human souls are created by God as intrinsically immortal, whereas others argue that the soul only becomes extrinsically immortal upon the reception of "eternal life" through *salvation. Either way, it is commonly agreed that all humans, whether righteous or wicked, are subject to physical death as a consequence of sin and thus are universally mortal as to their earthly life. Whatever *immortality humans possess is due to the will and power of God.

immutability. The characteristic of not experiencing change or development. Certain understandings of God posit the divine reality as incapable of experiencing change in any way. Some theologians, however, assert that this concept owes more to Greek philosophical influence than to explicit biblical teaching. Many contemporary theologians distinguish between God's eternally unchanging, faithful character and God's ability to respond in different ways to changing human beings in their temporal, earthly situation.

impassibility *(apatheia).* The characteristic, usually associated with God, of being unaffected by earthly, temporal circumstances, particularly the experience of suffering and its effects. Many contemporary theologians reject the idea of divine impassibility, suggesting that it reflects Greek philosophical, rather than biblical, concerns. However, the Bible clearly teaches that God cannot be swayed in any way to be unfaithful to what God has promised. Still, it is seemingly impossible to associate pure impassibility with God in light of the fact that Jesus Christ, as the fullest manifestation of God, experienced suffering on the cross.

impeccability. The characteristic of being unable to sin or being completely free from sin. Although true of the triune God, impeccability is more often specifically attributed to Jesus Christ in his earthly life and ministry. Although Jesus was fully human and therefore subject to the pressures of temptation as is any other human, Jesus is said to have been impeccable either because he was also fully God or because he resisted temptation.

imputation. A transfer of benefit or harm from one individual to another. In theology *imputation* may be used negatively to refer to the transfer of the sin and guilt of Adam to the rest of humankind. Positively, imputation refers to the righteousness of Christ being transferred to those who believe on him for *salvation.

incarnation. Fundamentally, *incarnation* is a theological assertion that in Jesus the eternal Word of God appeared in human form (Jn 1). Many theologians picture the incarnation as the voluntary and humble act of the second person of the *Trinity, God the Son, in taking upon himself full humanity and living a truly human life. The *orthodox doctrine of the incarnation asserts that in taking humanity upon himself, Christ did not experience a loss of his divine nature in any way but continued to be fully God. *See also hypostasis,* hypostatic union.

inclusivism. A theory of *salvation that suggests that although God saves people only on the merits of Christ, not all who are saved have consciously known of Jesus or heard the gospel. God saves those who, although they have not heard of Jesus, nevertheless respond to the best of their knowledge to the revelation of God available to them. This view stands in contrast to both *exclusivism, which suggests that God saves only those who consciously respond to the presentation of the gospel of Jesus Christ, and to *pluralism, which sees saving value in non-Christian religions.

individualism. A mindset of modern Western culture that emphasizes that meaning in life is found in a person's ability to think and make choices for her- or himself. In its radical form individualism defines a person as the sum total of her or his own preferences, thoughts and emotions without reference to any external relationships. In Western Christianity individualism predominated in the modern era and has had the unfortunate effect of making Christianity primarily a transaction between an individual and God, generally without sufficient emphasis on the believer's relationship with and responsibility to the larger faith community of the church.

indulgences. A practice of the medieval Roman Catholic Church that suggested that financial contributions to the church could ensure that a person who had died could be released from *purgatory (the place of torment) into heavenly bliss. Indulgences, among other practices, prompted Martin Luther to question the scriptural basis for many teachings of the medieval Roman Catholic Church. This in turn led to the Protestant *Reformation and Luther's emphasis on a person being declared righteous on the basis of faith in Christ alone without reference to meritorious human works of any kind.

inerrancy. The idea that Scripture is completely free from error. It is generally agreed by all theologians who use the term that *inerrancy* at least refers to the trustworthy and authoritative nature of Scripture as God's Word, which informs humankind of the need for and the way to *salvation. Some theologians, however, affirm that the Bible is also completely accurate in whatever it teaches about other subjects, such as science and history.

infallibility. The characteristic of being incapable of failing to accomplish a predetermined purpose. In Protestant theology infallibility is usually associated with Scripture. The Bible will not fail in its ultimate purpose of revealing God and the way of *salvation to humans. In Roman Catholic theology infallibility is also extended to the teaching of the church ("*magisterium" or "*dogma") under the authority of the pope as the chief teacher and earthly head of the body of Christ.

infralapsarian. *See* sublapsarianism, infralapsarianism.

inspiration. A term used by many theologians to designate the work of the Holy Spirit in enabling the human authors of the Bible to record what God desired to have written in the Scriptures. Theories explaining how God "superintended" the process of Scripture formation vary from dictation (the human authors wrote as secretaries, recording word for word what God said) to ecstatic writing (the human authors wrote at the peak of their human creativity). Most *evangelical theories of inspiration maintain that the Holy Spirit divinely guided the writing of Scripture, while at the same time allowing elements of the authors' culture and historical context to come through, at least in matters of style, grammar and choice of words.

intermediate state. The situation of those people who have died and who now await the future *resurrection. Major theories about the intermediate state proposed in the history of Christian theology include "soul sleep" (dead persons, whether believers or not, are completely unconscious); "restful bliss or conscious torment" (dead believers consciously experience the loving presence of Christ, while dead unbelievers consciously experience torment); and *purgatory (the Roman Catholic belief that dead persons experience degrees of suffering in order to purge them of their earthly sin). Some theologians deny the existence of an intermediate state, suggesting instead that those who die are ushered directly into eternity.

internal testimony of the Spirit *(testimonium Spiritus sancti internum)*. The working of the Holy Spirit in bringing about human confidence in the truthfulness of Scripture regarding God's promises of *salvation to all who exercise faith in Christ. The Word and the Spirit work together as a single testimony but in two manifestations: internally and externally. As the Scriptures are read, testifying to the work of Christ in bringing about salvation to those who believe (external), the Holy Spirit works within the believer to give a spiritual sense of the reality of faith (internal). The doctrine of the internal testimony has its origins in *Augustine and was especially affirmed by Protestant theologians during and after the *Reformation.

intuitionism. The philosophical theory that knowledge is gained partially, if not exclusively, by a direct mental awareness that does not come through any external senses. Thus intuitionism suggests that knowledge is not the result of observation by the sight, smell, touch, hearing or taste (*empiricism), nor is knowledge the result of using logical processes of the mind (rationalism).

Rather knowledge comes to the mind directly and apart from human rational and observational powers.

invisible church. A designation, dating perhaps to *Augustine, referring to the sum total of all genuine believers who have been united by the Holy Spirit into the body of Christ, whether living or dead. Unlike the *visible church, which is a historical, localized gathering of people who profess faith in Christ whether or not they are truly in Christ, the invisible church cannot be observed outwardly because its members are known only by God, who sees their internal faith and not merely their outward profession of faith. *See also* church.

Irenaeus (c. A.D. 130-200). An early Greek father of the church who served as a bishop, theologian and apologist and who wrote particularly against *Gnostic heresies of the day. Irenaeus is probably best known for proposing the doctrine of recapitulation, that is, the suggestion that Christ came to "sum up" (recapitulate) all that humans were intended to be, especially in light of all that was lost through the sin of Adam.

irenics. The practice of debating and discussing Christian doctrines with other Christians who are theologically *orthodox but with whom there are matters of genuine theological disagreement. It involves the friendly but rigorous task of doing theological reflection together within the community of faith. Irenics stands in contrast to *polemics, which is the practice of debating, discussing and refuting the positions of those who stand outside the accepted orthodox boundaries of Christian theology yet who insist on calling themselves Christian.

irresistible grace. A doctrine found in most *Calvinistic theologies that teaches that the Holy Spirit will work in the hearts of those whom God has chosen (the *elect) such that they cannot, or at least will not, resist the saving *grace God imparts. Most Calvinist theologians distinguish between God's general grace (given by God to all humans in the testimony of creation) and God's saving, effectual or efficacious grace (which is applied directly to the heart of persons such that they respond in faith and which is thereby irresistible).

J

judgment. In a broad sense, God's evaluation as to the rightness or wrongness of an act of a creature, whether human or angelic, using the standard of God's own righteous and holy character. In a more specific sense, *judgment* refers to the future event when God through Jesus Christ will judge all people, whether righteous or wicked, for their works done while on earth. The NT indicates that all people, whether Christian or not, will be judged according to their deeds; however, Christians will be accepted in light of the work of Christ on their behalf.

justice. In a general sense, the practice of giving reward or punishment for what is rightly due to a person or group of people. From a theological perspective, because God is sinless and holy, the justice of God demands that all persons and nations receive punishment because of their sin. In Christ the requirements of divine justice are met, and as a result, individuals can find mercy from God through Jesus Christ as the Holy Spirit draws them and convicts them of sin. In light of God's own just dealings with humankind, God also demands that humans deal justly with one another (Mt 23:23) and seek to release those under oppression, whether because of ethnic origin, gender or sociopolitical status (Is 58:6).

justification, justification by faith. A forensic (legal) term related to the idea of acquittal, *justification* refers to the divine act whereby God makes humans, who are sinful and therefore worthy of condemnation, acceptable before a God who is holy and righteous. More appropriately described as "justification by grace through faith," this key doctrine of the *Reformation asserts that a sinner is justified (pardoned from the punishment and condemnation of sin) and brought into relationship with God by faith in God's grace alone.

K

kairos. One of several Greek words for "time," *kairos* usually refers to a specific point of time as carrying crucial meaning for human life. This is in contrast to *kronos,* which designates the chrono-logical passing of time. Hence a "*kairos* moment" is an event in history in which God unveils some dimension of the eternal purposes of *salvation to humankind or an event that is central in God's dealings with humans. The fundamental *kairos* moment is the Christ event, that is, the life, death and *resurrection of Jesus, together with his future return (the *parousia).

Kant, Immanuel (1724-1804). One of the greatest philosophers of the Western tradition. Kant's thought grew out of the mindset of the *Enlightenment (which emphasized the primacy of reason in human life and in the pursuit of knowledge) and has had a profound affect on nineteenth- and twentieth-century philoso-phy and theology. Kant held that human knowing was dependent on the active mind and that theology should be conducted from the foundation of our sense of being morally conditioned.

kenosis, kenoticism. Derived from the use of the Greek verb *ekenōsen* (he emptied himself) in Philippians 2:7-11. *Kenosis* refers to the self-emptying of Christ in the incarnation, as well as his conscious acceptance of obedience to the divine will that led him to death by crucifixion. Many theologians see in the term a reference to Jesus' choice not to exercise the prerogatives and powers that were his by virtue of his divine nature. In the nineteenth century certain thinkers built this idea into a kenotic *Christology, which spoke of the incarnation as the self-emptying of the preexistent, eternal Son to become the human Jesus. This self-emptying involved the setting aside of certain divine attrib-utes, or at least the independent exercise of his divine powers.

kerygma. Literally, "proclamation," the term refers to the funda-mental NT message of the gospel of Jesus Christ (the content of the preached Word) or to the proclamation of this message, especially through preaching (the act of publicly proclaiming the Word). The basis for the *kerygma* lies in Jesus' own preaching (Mk 1:14-15), but theologians generally focus more specifically on the proclamation of the early church as it witnessed to the person and work of Jesus as the Christ.

Kierkegaard, Søren (1813-1855). Among the most influential modern philosophical and theological writers, Kierkegaard emphasized subjective truth and experience rather than universal ideals. His "*existential" dialectics dealt with the position of the individual human existing in the presence of God, thereby emphasizing the relation of the individual soul to God almost to the exclusion of the idea of Christian community. Kierkegaard likewise linked truth with the individual knowing subject rather than with the external object.

kingdom. The dynamic reign of God as sovereign over creation. Although the roots of the term lie in the OT, the Christian understanding arises more specifically from Jesus' proclamation of the inbreaking of God's rule. Hence the kingdom is God's divine, kingly reign as proclaimed and inaugurated by Jesus' life, ministry, death and *resurrection, and the subsequent outpouring of the Spirit into the world. In this sense Christ is reigning now, and the kingdom of God has arrived. At the same time the *church awaits the future consummation of the divine reign. This "already" and "not yet" dimension of the kingdom of God implies that it is both a given reality (or the divine power at work in the present) and a process that is moving toward its future fulfillment or completion.

koinōnia. A Greek word meaning "fellowship," "communion" or "sharing together." The term refers to the community or fellowship of Christian believers participating together in the life of Christ as made possible by the Spirit. This foundational shared participation in turn indicates the basic characteristics of the Christians' life together as a community of disciples.

L

laity. Literally, "people," the word refers technically to the whole people of God incorporated into the body of Christ. The term has come to refer to those who are nonordained as distinguished from ordained *clergy.

law, legalism. The *law* means variously the OT in general, the Torah (especially the Pentateuch or first five books of the Bible), the Ten Commandments or the several codes of conduct that identified Israel as set apart and in covenantal relationship with God. Jesus summarized the law with two commandments: to love God with heart, soul, mind and strength, and to love one's neighbor as oneself. Paul declares that the law is fulfilled in Jesus, who sets humans free from the law's penalty of death. *Legalism* is the attitude that identifies morality with the strict observance of laws or that views adherence to moral codes as defining the boundaries of a community. Religious legalism focuses on obedience to laws or moral codes based on the (misguided) assumption that such obedience is a means of gaining divine favor.

liberalism. A movement in nineteenth- and twentieth-century *Protestant circles that builds from the assumption that Christianity is reconcilable with the positive human aspirations, including the quest for autonomy. Liberalism desires to adapt religion to modern thought and culture. Consequently, it views divine love as realized primarily, if not totally, in love of one's neighbor and the *kingdom of God as a present reality found especially within an ethically transformed society. One of the significant early liberal theologians was Albrecht *Ritschl. *See also* postliberalism.

liberation theology. This term most often refers to a theological movement developed in the late 1960s in Latin America (where it continues to hold prominence). In attempting to unite theology and sociopolitical concerns, liberation theologians such as Gustavo Gutiérrez emphasize the scriptural theme of liberation, understood as the overcoming of poverty and oppression. Liberation theologies have also found expression among representatives of seemingly marginalized groups in North American society, including women, African Americans, Hispanics, Native Americans and Asian Americans.

limited atonement. Sometimes called "particular redemption," the view that Jesus' death secured *salvation for only a limited number of persons (the elect), in contrast to the idea that the work of the cross is intended for all humankind (as in "unlimited atonement"). This view resulted from the post-Reformation development of the doctrine of *election in Calvinist circles. Proponents claim that because not everyone is saved, God could not have intended that Christ die for everyone. *See also* atonement theories.

literalism. A strict adherence to the exact word or meaning, either in interpretation or translation, of the biblical text. Regarding interpretation, literalism generally attempts to understand the author's intent by pursuing the most plain, obvious meaning of the text as judged by the interpreter. In translation, the attempt is made to convey with utmost accuracy through the words of another language the actual meaning of the biblical text.

liturgy. The English word arises from the Greek term *leitourgia,* which was connected to the idea of sacrifice and designated the priestly service connected initially with the temple (e.g., Lk 1:23) and subsequently with Christian ministry and worship. Liturgy came to designate the church's official (or unofficial) public and corporate ritual of worship, including the *Eucharist (or Communion), baptism and other sacred acts. Certain ecclesiastical traditions (such as Roman Catholic, *Eastern Orthodox, *Anglican) follow a set pattern of worship (the liturgy), whereas many Protestant churches prefer a less structured style. This gives rise to the distinction sometimes made between "liturgical" and "nonliturgical" churches.

logical positivism. *See* positivism, logical positivism, logical empiricism.

logocentrism. The designation by postmodern philosophers such as Jacques Derrida for the philosophical method that looks to the *logos* (the word or written language) as the carrier of meaning. Derrida rejects the attendant philosophical assumption that human language is able to designate, signify or represent an *essence (or presence of being) that we can come to know.

Lord's Supper. A designation for the *sacrament or *ordinance of the church otherwise known as Communion or the *Eucharist. This designation, which is most widely used within the believers' churches, links the contemporary act with the final meal Jesus shared with his disciples on the evening preceding his crucifixion.

love. In the Christian tradition love (especially *agapē*) is an expression of the essential nature of God, the perfect characterization of the relationship between God and humans, and the supernatural virtue or character of God reflected in the Christian community in relation to God and one another as shaped by the indwelling Holy Spirit. This connection between love and God's own character gives rise to the Christian focus on love as the fundamental characteristic of Christian discipleship and hence of Christian *ethics. Many Christian thinkers suggest that the *essence of love is unconditional giving of oneself for the sake of others.

Lutheranism. The theological and ecclesiastical tradition based on the teachings of Martin Luther (1483-1546), who is credited with launching the *Reformation in Germany. Luther's "tower experience" convinced him that the essence of the gospel is that *justification comes only by the gift of God's grace appropriated by faith (*see sola gratia; sola fide*). According to Luther, God declares the sinner righteous through Jesus' death rather than through human merit or works. Faith entails trust in and acceptance of God's gift of *salvation through the "merits" of Christ.

M

magisterium. The prerogative of the church to proclaim and teach the good news about Jesus. In many church bodies the term refers more specifically to the group of persons, generally vocational theologians and church officials, who together possess the authority to determine the content of and to pass on to others the official doctrine, teachings and practices of the church. *Magisterium* is used in a more limited sense to refer to the authoritative teaching body within the Roman Catholic Church, consisting of the bishops under the authority of the pope. The bishops fulfill various kinds of "ordinary" magisterium in an ongoing manner. The "extraordinary" magisterium emerges when the bishops are assembled into a council or the pope proclaims some new *dogma (*ex cathedra*).

magisterial Reformation. The designation for the Lutheran, Zwinglian and Calvinist wings of the sixteenth-century Protestant movement, in contrast to the *Anabaptist wing (sometimes designated the *Radical Reformation). In contrast to the Anabaptist leaders, who acted apart from the sponsorship of political rulers, the magisterial Reformers were convinced that political power ought to be employed to advance the cause of ecclesiastical reform. *See also* Reformation.

Manichaeism. The third-century religion founded by the Iranian philosopher Mani, who believed he was the last and greatest prophet sent to perfect the Persian, Christian and Buddhist religions. Manichaeism is a form of dualistic *Gnosticism offering *salvation by knowledge. In practice it included strict *asceticism (especially in the form of discouraging involvement in physical pleasures) on the basis of the belief that the imperfect is subject to continual physical rebirth. Before his conversion *Augustine was a Manichaean for nine years.

Marcionism. The movement begun with Marcion in the second century, which rejected the validity of the OT witness for Christians because the God of the OT was believed to be incompatible with the loving God revealed through Jesus. Often persons who focus on the NT in their preaching or teaching and who overlook the OT as the "cradle" for Jesus and the Christian faith (and hence who fail to give proper credence to the "Jewishness" of Jesus and the early church) are accused of Marcionism.

Mariology. The theological teaching about Mary the mother of Jesus. The Roman Catholic Church has come to accept certain teachings about Mary that have developed through tradition as an essential part of Christian *dogma (essential beliefs enjoined on all Catholics). These dogmatic affirmations include Mary's *immaculate conception, perpetual virginity, sinlessness, plenitude of grace and bodily *assumption into heaven.

Marxism. Also called dialectical materialism, the political, social and economic principles espoused by Karl Marx, who held that the socioeconomic structures of a given society condition its basic values, laws, customs and beliefs. The theory and practice of Marxism include the labor theory of value and the goal of the establishment of a classless society. Marxism has influenced certain strands of contemporary theology, particularly *liberation theology.

materialism. A philosophical outlook that contends that physical matter is the only reality or category of existence, so that everything that exists is a manifestation of the material (rather than a manifestation of the mind). In more popular parlance, the term refers to pursuit of money and possessions as a central goal of human existence. *See also* monism.

medieval, medieval theology. Pertaining to the period generally described as the Middle Ages, which some date beginning as early as the seventh century and ending as late as the sixteenth. Medieval theology was chiefly concerned with systematizing and organizing Christian truth as it had been developed by the leading thinkers of the *patristic era. This led eventually to the writing of the great theological treatises that encompassed the entire body of Christian teaching. The flowering of medieval theology came in the so-called high Middle Ages (the twelfth and thirteenth centuries), especially in the work of Thomas *Aquinas, such as in his *Summa Theologica* (summary of theology).

memorialism. Originating with Ulrich *Zwingli, a view of the *Lord's Supper that sees the rite as symbolic, as representing (or memorializing) Christ's self-giving on the cross (together with his last supper with the disciples). In contrast to the idea of the *real presence espoused both by the medieval theologians and by Luther (e.g., the theories of *transubstantiation and *consubstantiation), memorialists believe that Christ's presence is not localized in the communion elements but within the gathered community of believers. Memorialists consider the word *is* in Christ's words, "This is my body. . . . This is my blood" (Mk 14:22, 24) to be figurative, so that it means "signifies" or "represents." Hence by this phrase Jesus was not referring literally to his physical body and blood but was indicating that the physical elements are symbols of his life that would be given for them.

Mennonites. Originally the followers of Menno Simons (1496-1561), a leader among the so-called *Anabaptists in the sixteenth century. In keeping with the *believers'-church tradition of which they are a part, Mennonite communities recognize no elaborate statements of common doctrine and reject the idea of a national church, infant baptism and the theory of the *real presence of Christ in the *Eucharist. They uphold personal and corporate piety through strict adherence to the NT. Generally, Mennonites are pacifists.

merit. Theologically, *merit* is a person's perceived right to be rewarded by God for works done on God's behalf. Although the Catholic tradition continues to uphold merit as a valid Christian category, the Reformers repudiated it, particularly in favor of the doctrine of *justification by grace through faith.

Messiah. A Hebrew term meaning "anointed one." The OT people of God came to anticipate a person anointed by the Spirit who would function once again as king and priest over Israel. Hence in Jewish (OT and intertestamental) theology, the Messiah was the person, whether supernatural or earthly, endowed with special powers and functions by God, who would appear as the divinely appointed, *eschatological deliverer and ruler of Israel. Although Jesus rarely used the title specifically for himself, the NT designation of Messiah (Greek *Christos*) belongs only to Jesus, both as a title and as a personal name. Jesus was the one who was truly anointed by the Holy Spirit, and as the bearer of the Spirit he has the prerogative to pour out the Spirit on his followers.

metanarrative. The idea that there is an overarching, all-embracing story of humankind into which all the more particular narratives fit (e.g., *salvation history). Christians believe that the biblical narrative of *creation-*Fall-*redemption-new creation is this all-embracing metanarrative, for the biblical story is the narrative of all humankind. In this sense the biblical narrative functions in Christian teaching as the central metanarrative.

metaphor, metaphorical theology. A metaphor is a figure of speech in which a word or phrase that has an accepted, literal meaning is used in place of another to suggest a likeness or similarity between them. Metaphorical theology holds that God can only be spoken about through metaphors. Thus we must use metaphors to name our experience of God (the "Transcendent"); consequently, God can be described only in relational terms (that is, through the relational language of metaphor). Furthermore, metaphorical theologians, such as Sallie McFague, generally claim that such metaphors are culturally conditioned representations created by the mind as we seek to make experience intelligible.

metaphysics. The philosophical exploration into the ultimate nature of reality lying beyond the merely physical (meta = beyond). Metaphysics deals with *ontological concerns, that is, with questions about what constitutes something as "real" or as having "being."

method in theology, methodology. A particular systematic procedure (or set of procedures), technique or mode of inquiry used in the development of a theological position. Systematic theologians generally treat matters of theological method in the opening sections of their treatises (the *prolegomenon). Such methodological questions often include: What is theology? What constitutes a valid, true or helpful theology? Why is theology important? Is theology a science? What forms the foundation of the task of engaging in theology? What are the sources (or what is the source) of theology? And what constitutes the proper way of constructing a theological system?

method of correlation. A theological method that seeks to correlate or bring together theological truth with contemporary philosophical or cultural questions. The theologian using this method believes that these questions provide the "point of contact" between the human quest for truth and the revealed truth of the Christian faith. According to Paul *Tillich (who may have coined the designation), philosophy raises questions and poses problems that reflect the existential concerns humans share. Theology in turn seeks to understand the questions and to answer them in ways that are both culturally relevant and faithful to the original Christian message.

Methodism. Originally a system of faith and practice established by John and Charles *Wesley and their followers in the eighteenth century. This evangelistic, revivalist movement expanded throughout Britain, the United States and other parts of the world. In early Methodism converts were incorporated into highly disciplined bands or societies that emphasized corporate confession, prayer, service and personal holiness. Modern Methodism reflects a strong commitment to practical social involvement. *See* Wesleyanism.

middle knowledge. The philosophical theory that asserts that

God knows all possible events and all theoretical truths, as well as all actual events and truths. Middle knowledge suggests that God knows not only what humans actually do but also what humans would do under hypothetical circumstances. For example, in the case of persons who die without hearing the gospel message, God knows how they would have responded had they heard it. Some theologians conclude that based on this middle knowledge, God will save those who remained beyond the pale of the gospel in this life but would have accepted Christ had the message come to them.

millennium, millennialism. Arising from the Latin word for "thousand," the *millennium* refers to the thousand-year reign of Christ mentioned in Revelation 20:1-8. There are basically three understandings as to what this text teaches: *premillennialism, *postmillennialism and *amillennialism. In contrast to amillennialists, who do not see the millennium as a specific period of history, both post- and premillennialists are technically millennialists in that both anticipate that the millennium will occur at some future time (or arrived in the recent past). Millennialism also goes by the term *chiliasm,* arising out of the biblical Greek word *chilias,* meaning "one thousand." In contemporary theology, chiliasm is often used in the narrower sense of referring to belief in the premillennial return of Christ.

modalism. Also called *Sabellianism, the trinitarian heresy that does not view Father, Son and Spirit as three particular "persons in relation" but merely as three modes or manifestations of the one divine person of God. Thus God comes in *salvation history as Father to create and give the law, as Son to redeem and as Spirit to impart grace.

modernism. The attempt to bring Christianity into harmony with the concerns of the modern era or modern people. Within Roman Catholicism, modernism was a liberal movement in the late nineteenth century aimed at bringing Catholic tradition into closer relation with (then) modern philosophical, historical, scientific and social views, especially by devaluing belief in the supernatural. *See also* liberalism.

modernity. The cultural worldview of the nineteenth and twentieth centuries, inherited from the *Enlightenment and reflective of its values and belief systems. Modernity is epitomized by the belief that through the exercise of reason alone we are capable of attaining knowledge, even knowledge of the divine, and that with such knowledge humans can progress, eventually even to the point of creating a utopian (or ideal) human order.

modes of being. The language used by the prominent twentieth-century theologian Karl *Barth to express the persons of the *Trinity. Barth was motivated by his reaction to the limitations of the modernized psychological understanding of *person*. Barth challenged the tritheistic idea of the Trinity as three distinct, personal centers of consciousness and will that stand apart from each other. He emphasized that the one God simultaneously exists in three self-differentiated "repetitions" or ways of being: Father, Son and Holy Spirit.

monarchianism. A movement in the second and third centuries that attempted to safeguard *monotheism and the unity (*mono-archē* = "one source") of the Godhead. By denying the personal reality of the Son and the Spirit as separate from the Father, however, this defensive attempt resulted in an antitrinitarian heresy. Two forms of monarchianism developed: *adoptionist, or dynamic monarchianism, which understood Jesus as merely a prophet filled with the Spirit and thus "adopted" by God; and *modalism (or *Sabellianism), which viewed Jesus as one of the modes through which the one God reveals himself to us.

monasticism. A way of life within the Catholic and *Eastern Orthodox traditions that emphasizes celibacy, life-in-community, poverty, common worship, silence and contemplation. The monastic movement spawned monasteries as places in which monks could live and work together, generally as cloistered from the larger society.

monism. Any antidualist philosophy that appeals to one unifying principle to explain all that is. In response to the metaphysical question "How many things are real or exist?" monism answers, "Only one reality or thing" or "One *kind* of thing with many different things within that category" (attributive monism). In effect, monism allows for no distinction between God and creation.

monotheism. The belief in one God *(mono-theos)* as opposed to belief in many gods (polytheism). Although monotheists may acknowledge the reality of other supernatural powers (such as angels and demons), they believe that all such powers are ultimately under the control or authority of the one God who alone is supreme. Monotheism in its various forms is the teaching of Judaism, Christianity and Islam.

Montanism. A second-century prophetic movement that emphasized the *imminent return of Christ and imposed a strict morality on the faithful as they waited and prepared for the end of the world. The designation *Montanism* arises from the leader of the movement, Montanus, who together with several women served as prophet to the group. Although its leaders did not intend their prophecies to undermine scriptural authority, the movement was nonetheless considered heretical by the emerging church authority. The church father *Tertullian eventually joined the Montanists.

moral argument (for God's existence). The argument first used by Immanuel *Kant, which claims that morality (humans' seeking the "highest good") presupposes the existence of God, who is both the lawgiver and the judge who will reward humankind's moral striving. More recently, C. S. Lewis offered a revision of the moral argument.

moral influence theory of the atonement. The view attributed to Peter Abelard that above all the cross is the grand display of God's love. In response to the love of God thus displayed, we in turn love God and live for God rather than continuing in sin.

mysticism. The belief and practice that seeks a personal, experiential (sometimes referred to as contemplative) knowledge of God by means of a direct, nonabstract and loving encounter or union with God. Although a psychophysical dimension (including visions, dreams or special revelation) may be part of the mystical experience, this dimension is not necessary. Instead, Christian mystics generally teach that the true test of the experience is the resulting fruit of the Spirit in the mystic's life.

myth. The term *myth* is most often associated with fable or with the historically inauthentic (fiction) rather than with truth and objective reality. Hence some people apply *myth* to any part of the Christian message that includes the supernatural or miraculous (*see* Bultmann; demythologizing). *Myth* can also be used to describe the true but transcendent or ineffable quality of God's revelation, which is beyond rational, linguistic description (*see* Brunner). *Myth* also connotes the language or imagery borrowed from the *cosmological/cosmogonical (creation) myths to speak of God.

N

narrative, narrative theology. Since the 1970s, a theological approach that utilizes the concept of story and the human person as storyteller (e.g., Gabriel Fackre, Hans Frei, Stanley Hauerwas, George Stroup) to provide the central motif for theological reflection. Narrative theologians claim that we construct our personal identity as our individual stories are joined with the transcendent story of the religious community and ultimately with the overarching narrative of *salvation history.

naturalism, natural theology. *Naturalism* sometimes refers to a form of *atheism and *materialism that maintains that the "natural" universe (composed of energy and matter and based on natural laws) is the sum total of reality, thereby negating human freedom, absolute values and, ultimately, *existential meaning. As an ethical theory naturalism suggests that ethical judgments arise out of or are based in the universe itself or "the way things naturally are." Natural theology maintains that humans can attain particular knowledge about God through human reason by observing the created order as one locus of divine *revelation.

natural headship. The theory about original sin, sometimes attributed to *Augustine, that declares that Adam is the "natural head" of humankind in that he is the father of the entire race. This observation, in turn, suggests how it is that all humans are guilty for Adam's sin: Because Adam is the progenitor of all, all humans were present in Adam when he sinned.

neo-orthodoxy. An early twentieth-century Protestant movement (involving, among others, Karl *Barth, Emil *Brunner and Reinhold and H. Richard *Niebuhr) borne out of a sense that Protestant *liberalism had illegitimately accomodated the gospel to modern science and culture, and in the process had lost the classical focus on the *transcendence of God as well as the Word of God. In this situation neo-orthodox thinkers promoted a return to the basic principles of *Reformation theology and the early church (especially the primacy of Scripture, human depravity and God's work in Christ) as the basis for proclaiming the gospel in the contemporary context, while taking seriously the *Enlightenment critique of *orthodoxy and rejecting Protestant *scholasticism. Neo-orthodox theologians often used a *dialectical approach, which sought theological insight through the juxtaposing of seemingly opposing formulations held together as paradoxically true (e.g., humans are fallen and depraved, yet free and accountable before God).

Neo-Platonism. The last stage of Greek philosophy (identified with Plotinus), which greatly influenced certain early church thinkers, particularly *Origen and *Augustine. Neo-Platonists taught that everything emanates (flows) from the transcendent principle of the One and is destined to return to the One through a process of purification.

Nestorianism. Condemned by the *Council of Ephesus (A.D. 431), the view held by Nestorius, bishop of Constantinople, that although Jesus Christ was one person (God and man united), his two natures (one human and one divine) existed side by side and hence were separable. One consequence of this view was that Jesus' suffering for humankind was seen as an act of Jesus in his humanity but not in his deity.

Nicene Creed. Originally the theological confession resulting from the first *Council of Nicaea (A.D. 325), convened by the emperor Constantine to resolve church divisions related to the Arian controversy (*see* Arianism). The creed reflects the teaching that the Son is of one substance with the Father (*see homoousios*). The Nicene Creed recited in churches today resembles the original, but having been revamped at the Council of Constantinople (A.D. 381), the current version is longer and excludes certain original phrases.

Niebuhr, Reinhold (1892-1971). One of the most prominent voices in American theology throughout the middle years of the twentieth century. His rejection of *liberalism drew Niebuhr to focus attention on Christian *anthropology, which he believed presented the human person as both fallen and free. Niebuhr was likewise interested in the relevance of Christianity for contemporary social problems. Against what he saw as the "moral utopianism" (unbridled optimism) of liberalism, he proposed "Christian Realism," that is, the attempt to bring about what was realistically possible, namely, a more just situation than was present previously (proximate justice) rather than inaugurate the perfect social order, which he deemed unattainable due to our fallenness. *See* neo-orthodoxy.

nihilism. In general, the complete rejection of (and in the extreme, the destruction of) beliefs and values associated with moral and traditional social structures. Philosophically, nihilism represents an attitude of total skepticism regarding objective truth claims. Nihilism views knowledge as dependent on sensory experience alone, so that moral and theological claims are meaningless.

noetic. Relating to, based on or having to do with the intellect or the process of knowing.

nominalism. The theory of knowledge that denies the objective reality of universal principles, maintaining that "universals" are mere concepts with no reality apart from their existence in the mind of the individual. This theory is sometimes attributed to the medieval thinker William of Occam (*see* Occam's razor).

noncompatibilism. *See* compatibilism.

nonfoundationalism. The view that suggests that knowledge does not arise as conclusions from certain nondebatable first principles (*see* foundationalism). Instead, nonfoundationalists argue that knowledge consists of a set of beliefs that fit together in some interconnected pattern (e.g., a "web of belief") and hence mutually support each other.

norm. In *ethics an authoritative standard or principle of right action that is binding on members of a group. Norms serve to control, regulate or guide what is considered acceptable behavior or attitudes for a group, thus contributing to its overall definition. In theology a norm is what gives shape to and determines the content of doctrinal formulations. Protestants generally appeal to one norm, Scripture, as standing above all others. Thus the Bible becomes the "norming norm" *(norma normans)* for theological reflection and construction.

notitia. Latin for knowledge of, or acquaintance with, something or someone. In theology *notitia* came to refer to one aspect of faith (the others being **assensus* and **fiducia*). To believe in Christ a person must first become acquainted with the gospel message.

numinous. Adopted from the Latin word *numen,* a word coined by German theologian Rudolph Otto to describe the core of religious experience as an encounter with the presence of "the holy." The numinous includes aspects of reason and morality, and because the numinous is "felt," it can be described but not strictly defined.

O

Occam's (Okham's) razor. One of the main axioms of nominalist philosopher William of Occam (c. 1300-1349), namely, that principles employed to explain any phenomenon should not be multiplied without necessity. In the modern era Occam's razor was used to eliminate the supernatural from view. Hence critics argued, for example, that we need no longer appeal to demonic possession to explain what is better referred to as some purely human malady such as epilepsy or mental illness.

oikonomia. Greek for "economy" or "administration." In theology the term refers to *salvation history or to God's providential plan and care (administration) of creation. More specifically, *oikonomia* has become synonymous with the main events in God's plan of salvation, particularly Christ's *incarnation and the sending of the Spirit.

omnipotence. The attribute that refers to God's ability to do whatever is consistent with God's own character and being in effecting the divine plan for creation. God's omnipotence is primarily demonstrated in God's overturning evil for good. This is especially evident in the death of Jesus, which although it was the act of malicious people, has become God's means of human *salvation.

omnipresence. The attribute that refers to God's being present everywhere in creation at the same time. Perhaps omnipresence more correctly suggests that all things are present to God. As a result there is nowhere in the universe that lies beyond the cognition (and care) of God.

omniscience. The attribute that denotes God's knowing all things. Omniscience means that all events are present to the divine mind; that is, God has direct cognition of everything in creation.

ontological argument. An argument for the existence of God that argues from the idea of God itself to the reality of God. It was attributed first to *Anselm and later to Descartes, who declared that because God is by definition "the most perfect being," God must exist; otherwise God would lack one perfection, namely, existence.

ontology. The branch of *metaphysics concerned with the nature of being. To speak of something as ontological is to refer to its essential nature, as opposed to its epistemological aspects. Ontology, therefore, focuses on being and *essence, in contrast to *epistemology, which speaks about how humans come to know something.

ordinance. Literally, an authoritative *decree or *law. Certain *free-church groups (such as the Baptists) refer to baptism and the *Lord's Supper as ordinances rather than *sacraments. In so doing they highlight the voluntary nature of these rites as having been ordained (commanded) by Christ.

ordination. Latin, meaning "to set in order" and later, "to appoint to office." *Ordination* most often refers to the appointment to an official ministerial capacity, often accompanied by the laying on of hands. Ordination in the Roman Catholic and Orthodox traditions is considered a *sacrament. Most churches ordain persons to pastoral leadership and service. Some churches also ordain persons to other offices, such as bishops (e.g., Catholics and *Anglicans) or *deacons (certain Baptists). Occasionally the term is associated with God's *election and *predestination.

ordo salutis. Latin, meaning "order of salvation," that is, the succession of events in God's salvific program. Although both the Catholic and Reformed traditions believe that *salvation comes only through Christ, they diverge dramatically regarding the *ordo salutis.* The *ordo salutis* of the *Reformed tradition includes such matters as effectual calling, *regeneration, *faith, *justification, *sanctification and *glorification. The Roman Catholic Church, in contrast, "dispenses grace" through the ordered *sacraments of baptism and confirmation, the *Eucharist, penance, either marriage or ordination, and the rite of healing, known in the past as extreme unction (the preparatory rite for death).

Origen (A.D. 185-254). A theologian and biblical scholar of the early Greek church, Origen vigorously defended the *orthodox Christian faith both in his speaking and in his monumental works. However, some of his theological speculations and approaches to Scripture led Origen to be declared a heretic in A.D. 553 by the Second Council of Constantinople. His conflicting trinitarian views laid foundations both for *Arianism and for future orthodox trinitarian theology. He is perhaps best known for his idea of "the eternal generation of the Son"; that is, throughout all eternity, the Father generates the Son. Rather than an act in time, this generation is an eternal act.

original sin, original righteousness (justice). Strictly speaking, original sin is the state of alienation from God into which all humans are born. Original righteousness (or original justice), in contrast, is the state of innocence in which Adam and Eve are thought to have existed before their fall into sin. Thus, because they had not yet disobeyed God, the first humans were righteous (without sin) in God's sight. Historically, original sin was connected to the discussion about the manner in which Adam's sin affects all humans, such as through the transmission of Adam's fallen nature or through God's imputation (crediting) of Adam's sin.

orthodoxy. Literally, "right praise" or "right belief" (as opposed to *heresy). Being orthodox implies being characterized by consistency in belief and worship with the Christian faith (in the Catholic tradition, consistency with the church) as witnessed to in Scripture, the early Christian writers and the official teachings, *creeds and *liturgy of the church. Orthodoxy is sometimes used in a narrower sense to refer to the *Eastern Orthodox tradition.

ousia. Greek for "substance" or "being." Trinitarian thought suggests that the Son derives his *ousia* from the Father, and yet what the Son is so the Father is exactly (*see homoousios*). In their formulation of the doctrine of the *Trinity, the *Cappadocian fathers declared that God was one *ousia* but three *hypostaseis*.

P

panentheism. The belief that God's being includes and permeates the entire universe so that everything exists in God. In contrast to *pantheism, panentheists declare that God's being is greater than and not exhausted by the universe. God is affected by each event in the universe, and thus God's knowledge must change and grow. However, God simultaneously retains personal integrity and complete reality.

pantheism. Greek for "everything is God," the belief that God and the universe are essentially identical. More specifically, *pantheism* is the designation for the understanding of the close connection between the world and the divine reality found in certain religions, including Hinduism. One variety of pantheism speaks of God as the "soul" of the universe, which is thought to be God's "body." Pantheistic religions often suggest that our experience of being disconnected from each other and from the divine is merely an illusion.

paradigm, paradigm shift. A paradigm is a conscious or unconscious structure of thought, belief and action. A paradigm shift is a change within this structure that results in the ability to perceive and consider things differently and thus to respond in a radically new or different manner. Through the writings of the twentieth-century American philosopher of science Thomas Kuhn, these terms have gained widespread use.

paradox. An apparent contradiction. A paradox may come in the form of a seemingly self-contradictory statement, in multiple statements that are mutually contradictory or by way of a statement that stands in contradiction to common sense or to a commonly held position. The Christian faith affirms several paradoxes—independent truths that seem irreconcilable to others and yet are held together by faith. One often-cited example is the belief that Jesus is fully divine yet fully human. Theologians often seek to pierce into these seemingly paradoxical aspects of the faith.

parousia. A Greek word used to refer to the second coming of Jesus Christ at the end of history. Literally, the term means "presence." Hence it designates Christ's return as the point at which he will be fully present to the world or his presence will be fully revealed.

patripassianism. Derived from the Greek words *patēr* (father) and *paschō* (to suffer), the term refers to an early type of *modalism that suggested that the one God (the Father) became incarnate in the form of the Son, was born of a virgin and suffered and died on the cross. This belief was declared heretical by the early church.

patristic era. From the Greek *patēr*, a term pertaining to the first few centuries of the church after the writing of the NT or to the early church fathers or writers of that period (generally A.D. 100-750). The patristic era began after the death of the apostles and was followed by the Middle Ages. Important patristic authors include such luminaries as *Irenaeus, *Origen, *Tertullian, the *Cappadocian fathers and *Augustine.

pedobaptism, paedobaptism (infant baptism). The practice of baptizing infants or children who are deemed not old enough to verbalize faith in Christ. There are several conceptions of the significance of infant baptism. Some Christians view the act as effecting *regeneration; others see it as the symbol of God's grace extended to the infant prior to personal response; others suggest that, like *circumcision in the OT, infant baptism marks an infant as a member of the *covenant community.

Pelagianism. The teaching of British monk Pelagius (c. 354–415), who supposedly declared that human effort and merit could bring about *salvation without divine grace. Pelagius was vigorously opposed by the church father *Augustine.

penal-substitution theory of the atonement. The view that speaks of sin as the breaking of God's law, for which the penalty is death. Hence on the cross Christ suffered the death penalty in the sinner's place and so appeased the wrath of God. This theory was first proposed in the *Reformation and later became the most widely held view among Protestants, especially *evangelicals, in Britain and the United States.

penance. In the Catholic tradition, the *sacrament of *reconciliation by which the penitent person is reconciled to God and the church through the forgiveness of sin. Often such reconciliation comes after the penitent sinner performs some prescribed act as an indication of repentance.

Pentecost, Pentecostalism. Originally the culmination of the OT Feast of Weeks, the church celebrates Pentecost as the anniversary of the coming of the Holy Spirit on the disciples fifty days after Jesus' *resurrection. Pentecostalism is a movement that began in the early twentieth century that emphasizes a postconversion "baptism in the Holy Spirit" for all believers, with *glossolalia (speaking in tongues) as the initial evidence of such baptism. Historically, Pentecostals have been a missionary-minded people, due in part to the fact that the first Pentecostals taught that one central purpose of baptism in the Spirit was to endow the believer with power for evangelism.

perichoresis. *See* circumincession.

perseverance of the saints. The mandate in Scripture to remain steadfast in the love of God and to patiently endure hardship, particularly in the face of persecution. In *Calvinist theology the perseverance (or preservation) of the saints refers to the belief that those who are truly among the elect will remain faithful to the end. In recent *evangelical theology a discussion has emerged as to how to balance the doctrine of eternal security (everyone who has accepted Christ as Savior will enjoy eternity with God regardless of postconversion personal conduct) with the biblical call to believers to persevere, that is, not to disobey or fall away from faith. *See also* Arminianism, Arminius; Calvinism, John Calvin.

person. Used of humans to denote a living being with the capacity for freedom, consciousness and relationships; of God as similarly yet preeminently personal; and of the three members of the *Trinity. When referring to the triune personhood of God, *person* does not have any similarity to the contemporary psychological understanding, nor does it connote three separate Gods. Instead, the trinitarian persons are relational in their personhood.

phenomenology. A philosophical movement of the twentieth century associated with Edmund Husserl and his followers. Phenomenology initially focused on *epistemology, that is, how we gain knowledge of *essences or the essential features of the world (abstract properties) on the basis of our perceptions of concrete realities (particular instances of those properties). Phenomenologists later turned their attention to the essences of human mental acts. Consequently phenomenology came to be associated with the study of the development of human consciousness and self-awareness.

pietism. A Bible-oriented, experiential approach to Christian life that emphasizes personal appropriation of faith and a lifestyle of holiness as more important than the formal structures of theology (doctrine) and church order. Initially Pietism was a movement within the Lutheran Church in Germany that sought to correct the focus on mere assent to doctrine, which the Pietists believed led to "dead orthodoxy." Philipp Jacob Spener (1635-1705) is often cited as the father of German Pietism. Spener sought to bring about change in the church by founding small groups of pious believers *(collegia pietatis)* who met for mutual edification.

Platonism. The philosophical system of the Greek philosopher Plato, which has immeasurably influenced Western (including Christian) thought. Plato's philosophy rests primarily on his concept of forms, *cosmology and *immortality. According to Plato, actual created things are imperfect copies of transcendent, objective and eternal "forms," the highest of which is the form of the Good. Human knowledge is innate and can be apprehended by rational reflection and Socratic "extraction." At death the body releases the imprisoned soul, which is then able to contemplate truth in its pure form.

plenary inspiration. A late-*Reformation view of biblical inspiration that holds that God is the ultimate author of the Bible in its entirety. That is, God's superintending work in inspiration extends to the whole Bible and to each part of the Bible. Plenary inspiration guarantees that all that the church has come to affirm as Scripture is both authoritative and helpful for Christian belief and practice.

pluralism. The advocacy and embrace of a social system that promotes the autonomy and ongoing development of diverse religious, ethnic, racial and social groups within the system. In theology, pluralism suggests that there are many paths to and expressions of truth about God and several equally valid means to *salvation.

pneumatology. The division of Christian doctrine dealing with the Holy Spirit. The word arises from the Greek words _pneuma_ (spirit) and _logos_ (the teaching about). Pneumatology explores the person and work of the Spirit, especially the Spirit's involvement in human *salvation.

point of contact. A term made famous by the debate between *Barth and *Brunner regarding whether or not there is a natural link through which the gospel can reach the sinful human individual. Barth contended that faith was created by the preaching of the Word and hence that there was no natural point of contact, whereas Brunner held that a natural link, such as in a person's sense of guilt, could be found.

polemics. The art of disputation or controversy (the defense of a thesis by formal logic). A polemic can also be the aggressive refutation of another position or principle. In theology _polemics_ often refers to the attempt to show the superiority of Christian teaching over its rivals by means of a systematic, ordered delineation of the Christian belief system (a *systematic theology) that shows the internal consistency of Christian doctrine as well as its congruence with human knowledge as a whole. _See also_ irenics.

positivism, logical positivism, logical empiricism. Positivism is the philosophical position that asserts that we can attain no knowledge of anything except what is directly apprehended by the senses. Thus "positive knowledge" arises through science in contrast to speculation, which is associated with *metaphysics and theology. _Logical_ positivism became an antimetaphysical position within modern philosophy that suggests that the central function of philosophy is to analyze language. Using scientific inquiry as the paradigm of human knowledge, logical positivists dismissed metaphysical statements as nonsensical.

posse peccare, posse non peccare. See impeccability; sinlessness of Christ.

postliberalism. The late-twentieth-century theological movement that refutes the reliance on human experience displayed by the older *liberalism and restores the idea of a community's tradition as a controlling influence in theology. Postliberalism was initially associated with thinkers such as George Lindbeck, who rejected both the *fundamentalist and liberal understandings of the nature of doctrine (as either objectively true propositions or expressions of subjective religious experience) in favor of the view that sees doctrine as the "ground rules" of a religious community.

postmillennialism. The view that Christ's second coming will follow the *millennium; that is, his return is postmillennial. Postmillennialists assert that the millennium will come by the spiritual and moral influence of Christian preaching and teaching in the world. This will result in increased *conversions, a more important role of the church in the world, earthly prosperity, the resolution of social ills and a general adoption of Christian values. Evil will diminish until the time of Christ's second coming, which will mark as well the *resurrection of the dead and the last *judgment.

postmodernism. A term used to designate a variety of intellectual and cultural developments in late-twentieth-century Western society. The *postmodern ethos is characterized by a rejection of modernist values and a mistrust of the supposedly universal rational principles developed in the *Enlightenment era. Postmoderns generally embrace *pluralism and place value in the diversity of worldviews and religions that characterizes contemporary society.

postmortem evangelism. The belief that the gospel message is somehow made available after death to persons who had never heard the good news in this life. These persons are then saved or lost on the basis of their response to the gospel.

pragmatism. The philosophical system that assumes that every truth or idea has practical consequences and that these practical consequences are a critical test of its truthfulness. Some pragmatists add that there are no transcendental sources of truth; therefore, truth and values are relative to their usefulness to either individuals or societies.

praxis, orthopraxy. Reflective, responsive action or the practical expression of the knowledge gained through one's concrete experience and reflection on it. Orthopraxy, literally meaning "right practice," is living out the known and experienced truth of the Christian faith in love and justice.

predestination. The sovereign determination and foreknowledge of God. Some theologians connect divine predestination with the central events of *salvation history, especially the death of Jesus as foreordained by God. In *Calvinist theology the doctrine of predestination more specifically holds that God has from all eternity chosen specific people to bring into eternal communion with himself. Some Calvinists add that God has also predestined (or ordained) the rest of humankind for *damnation.

preexistence (of the soul). The Platonic view, taken up by *Origen and other Greek fathers, that the soul exists with God prior to birth and that it is assigned a body (through which it becomes polluted) as a penalty for its sin of looking toward the earth.

premillennialism. The view that the *millennium follows the return of Christ, which therefore makes his return "premillennial." In the teaching of some premillennialists the millennium will begin supernaturally and cataclysmically, preceded by signs of apostasy, worldwide preaching of the gospel, war, famine, earthquakes, the coming of the *antichrist and the great *tribulation. Jesus will then return and rule on the earth with his saints for one thousand years, during which time peace will reign, the natural world will no longer be cursed and evil will be suppressed. After a final rebellion, God will crush evil forever; judge the resurrected, nonbelieving dead; and establish heaven and hell.

presuppositionalism. A variety of classical *evangelical apologetics often associated with Cornelius Van Til. Presuppositionalists assert that any system of belief is built on certain foundational presuppositions (unprovable assertions that must be believed to make experience meaningful). As a result, the best means of Christian apologetics is not to prove certain specific assertions such as the existence of God, the historicity of the *resurrection or the authority of the Bible. Instead the presuppositionalist Christian apologist explores the foundational presuppositions of competing belief systems with the goal of showing that human experience makes sense (or has meaning) most clearly when viewed in the light of the foundational teachings of the Christian faith.

prevenient grace. A designation of the priority of God's gracious initiative on behalf of humans. Hence the term refers to the gracious action of God, displayed in the person and work of Christ but present in the lives of human beings through the agency of the Holy Spirit, which precedes all human response to God's initiative. Calvinists view prevenient grace as that aspect of special grace by which God redeems, sanctifies and glorifies the believer; hence, it is bestowed only on those whom God elects to eternal life through faith in Jesus Christ. For *Wesley (and consequently for many *Arminians) prevenient grace is the Holy Spirit's work in the hearts of all people, which gives them the freedom to say yes to the gospel; thus prevenient grace can be accepted or rejected, but *justification cannot be achieved without it.

priesthood of believers. The *Reformation principle that declares that the privilege and freedom of all believing Christians is to stand before God in personal communion through Christ, directly receiving forgiveness without the necessary recourse to human intermediaries. As priests (1 Pet 2:5, 9), believers directly offer sacrifices of praise and thanksgiving to God and minister to the needs of others. Ordained pastors, in turn, are not different from other believers in spiritual status but only in function and appointment.

process theology. A twentieth-century theology based on the philosophy of Alfred North Whitehead that presents a dipolar God who is integrally involved in the endless process of the world through two natures: the "primordial," transcendent nature, wherein lies God's timeless perfection of character, and the "consequent," immanent nature, by which God is part of the changing cosmic process. Proponents include John B. Cobb Jr., Charles Hartshorne and Marjorie Suchocki.

procession. A term in Christian trinitarian thought that designates the way the Son and Spirit originate from the Father. The Son's procession from the Father is called *generation,* or *filiation,* whereas the procession of the Spirit from the Father (and the Son, in Western theology) is called *spiration.*

progressive revelation. The belief that God's self-disclosure forms a progression from the OT era to the NT era. Hence what is known about God on the basis of Jesus Christ is more complete than what was given through the Law and the Prophets. Progressive revelation implies that the OT ought to be understood in the light of the fuller teaching found in the NT.

prolegomenon. Prefatory remarks: a formal essay or critical discussion serving to introduce and interpret an extended work. In theology *prolegomenon* refers to the methodological questions generally found in the opening sections of a *systematic theology, dealing with the nature and task of theology and perhaps with the nature and focal point of revelation. *See also* method in theology, methodology.

prolepsis. An eschatological outlook that treats a future act or development as presently existing or already accomplished. A proleptic act is an eschatological occurrence happening within history prior to the end. Hence Jesus' resurrection is a prolepsis of the general resurrection that marks the end of the present age. *See also* eschaton, eschatology.

propitiation. An offering that turns away the *wrath of God directed against sin. According to the NT, God has provided the offering that removes the divine wrath, for in love the Father sent the Son to be the propitiation (or atoning sacrifice) for human sin (1 Jn 4:10). *See also* expiation.

proposition, propositionalism. A proposition is a meaningful, logical statement (or assertion) that can be confirmed in some manner, such as by sensory observation, and so can be subjected to scientific inquiry. Propositionalism presents and defends theological truths by setting them forth as a series of propositions that can be reasonably demonstrated to be true. Propositionalism serves as an important reminder that the Christian faith has a rational and, hence, scientifically demonstrable dimension. Critics accuse propositionalists of reducing the faith to a cognitive level and thereby missing the sense of wonder, awe and mystery about God and *salvation; the importance of the affective, emotive and intuitive dimensions of human life; and the importance of the practical outworking of Christian commitment in a life of service to God and others.

prosōpon. Greek for "face" or "appearance."

Protestantism, Protestant principle. Protestantism is the product of the "protestation" movement within Christianity that originated in the sixteenth-century *Reformation and was later focused in the main Protestant traditions (*Lutheran, *Calvinist/Presbyterian and *Anglican/Episcopalian). Because Protestants emphasized the primacy of Scripture against the Roman Catholic elevation of tradition alongside the Bible, the Protestant principle suggests that believers ought to read and seek to understand the Scriptures, and that church practice ought to be continually subjected to the scrutiny of Scripture. The Protestant principle declares that the final authority in the church is the Holy Spirit speaking through the Scriptures.

providence. Although *providence* is not a biblical term, both the OT and NT set forth an understanding of God's gracious outworking of the divine purpose in Christ within the created order in human history. The world and humanity are not ruled by chance or by fate but by God, who directs history and creation toward an ultimate goal. Providence therefore refers to God's superintending activity over human actions and human history, bringing creation to its divinely determined goal.

purgatory. In Catholic theology, the place of purification and maturation that one may need to enter after death before the perfected soul attains the "beatific vision"—that is, perfectly "seeing" and "knowing" the triune God. Protestants have generally rejected the concept as having no basis in Scripture and as denying the significance and finality of mortal life on earth.

Puritanism. A reform movement that originally sought to "purify" the Church of England after the English Reformation. Eventually Puritanism focused on purification of both individuals and society through the reform of church and state according to biblical principles. The Puritans held to a *covenantal theology and the conviction that Scripture was authoritative for personal behavior and church organization.

Q

quest of the historical Jesus. The nineteenth-century movement that sought to separate and distinguish the man Jesus of Nazareth from the Christ of faith as proclaimed by the church. The proponents of this quest concluded that the "historical" (non-supernatural) Jesus never made any messianic claim, never predicted his death or resurrection and never instituted the *sacraments now followed by the church. Instead the biblical stories that assign these acts to Jesus are nonhistorical "*myths" that, together with certain philosophical and theological claims set forth in the NT documents, were projected onto him by his disciples, the Gospel writers and the early church. The true historical Jesus, in contrast, preached a simple, largely ethical message as capsulized in the dictum of the "fatherhood of God" and the "brotherhood of humankind."

R

Radical Reformation. Also known as the left wing of the Reformation or the Third Reformation, this phrase designates the loose coalition of reforming groups that did not wish to be identified with the *magisterial reformation of *Zwingli, Luther and Calvin. The three main groups that made up the Radical Reformation are the *Anabaptists, the spiritualists and the evangelical rationalists. These groups shared a common disappointment with much of Protestantism. As a result, they rejected and went beyond some of the doctrines and institutions of the traditional Reformation churches. *See also* Calvinism, John Calvin; Lutheranism.

ransom theory of the atonement. The view that through human sin people rightfully belong to, or come under, the authority of Satan and that to remedy this situation God offered his Son as a ransom in exchange for humankind. But because Jesus could not be kept in hell, he rose on the third day, thereby causing Satan to lose those he held captive. This theory was widely taught during the *patristic era. *See also* atonement.

rapture. From the Latin *rapio* (caught up), the belief that the church will be caught up (Greek *harpazo,* 1 Thess 4:17) and united with Christ at his second coming. One point of contention among theologians is the time of the rapture, especially in relation to the great *tribulation period associated with the end of the age. The views regarding the related timing of these events lead to the designations pre-, mid- and posttribulationists for the views that the rapture occurs prior to, during or at the end of the tribulation. Some theologians view the rapture as a biblical image referring to the church's greeting the returning Christ.

reader-response theory of hermeneutics. A postmodern form of literary criticism that explores the capacity of the biblical texts to shape, revise or confirm the expectations readers bring to their reading of the text. This approach challenges the assumption of much of modern *hermeneutics that the main task of exegesis is to approach a text as a disinterested exegete and to determine, through the use of scientific strategies of interpretation, the intent of the original author of the text. Reader-response theorists, in contrast, maintain that the reader and the text are interdependent. What is important then is not so much the intent of the original author of the text but the "conversation" between reader and text that emerges in the reading of the text.

real presence of Christ in the Eucharist. The belief that Jesus Christ is actually physically and sacramentally present in the bread and the wine at the Lord's Table, or Holy Communion. The biblical basis for this view includes a literal understanding of Jesus' words of institution, "This is my body. . . . This is my blood" (Mk 14:22, 24) as well as the supposed allusion to the *Eucharist in Jesus' bread-of-life discourse (Jn 6:53-58). The real presence is taught by Lutherans and Roman Catholics (with substantial differences). *See also* consubstantiation; transubstantiation.

realism. A philosophical mindset that maintains that "universals" have a separate reality from and exist outside of the the mind. Although the proposal itself goes back to *Plato, it became theologically important in the Middle Ages as a heated debate emerged between realists and the nominalists. The realists maintained that properties (e.g., whiteness as a property of snow) exist independently of our thought, just as objects do. Consequently, for realists God's attributes (e.g., love and holiness) also have independent existence, just as God does. *See also* nominalism.

reconciliation. A change in relationship or attitude from enmity to peace; the cessation of hostility in attitude or action. Reconciliation is a central doctrine of Christianity. Specifically, in Christ God reconciled the sinful, hostile world to himself by Christ's taking upon himself the cost of our hostility and enmity, thereby setting the world free to restored union with God (2 Cor 5:19). The foundational assumption of the gospel is that only God can bear and remove the consequences of human enmity toward God and the resulting separation from God; therefore God alone can effect this change in relationship.

reconstructionism. A variety of contemporary *postmillennialism that asserts that our Christian duty moves beyond individual moral holiness to include a public, social responsibility to force society to obey the divine law revealed in the Bible through such means as government legislation. On the basis of an appeal to the idea of "dominion" (our human calling to exercise dominion over the earth), reconstructionists set as their goal the establishment of a Christian republic in which God's law rules.

redaction criticism. An approach to biblical interpretation focusing on the literary, theological contributions of the biblical authors by analyzing the way they modified their sources to arrive creatively and purposefully at their own special emphases.

redemption. The process by which sinful humans are "bought back" from the bondage of sin into relationship with God through grace by the "payment" of Jesus' death. Redemption is one of the pictures or metaphors that the NT uses to give insight into God's gracious saving work in Jesus.

Reformation. The general term for the period of massive ecclesial and theological change in Western Christianity that had its roots as early as the fourteenth century and lasted into the seventeenth century. The Reformation refers more specifically to the break with medieval Roman Catholicism launched in the sixteenth century by such luminaries as Martin *Luther, Ulrich *Zwingli and John *Calvin, who protested against what they perceived as the overall degeneracy of the Roman Church and its departure from what the Reformers saw as the faith of the apostles and early church fathers.

Reformed tradition, Reformed theology. The tradition and theological framework that grew out of the teachings of John *Calvin and Ulrich *Zwingli, as distinct from the *Lutheran and *Anabaptist traditions. Reformed theology focuses foundationally on God's glory and often emphasizes divine sovereignty as a crucial beginning point for theological reflection.

regeneration. A biblical motif of *salvation that emphasizes the rebirth or re-creation of fallen human beings by the indwelling Holy Spirit. One central biblical text depicting salvation as regeneration is Jesus' conversation with Nicodemus in which he emphasized the necessity of being "born again" (Jn 3:1-21).

reincarnation. The belief that human souls individually migrate from one body to another through a succession of lives until complete purification is achieved and they are finally joined to the ultimate reality, God. Although taught by the Greek philosopher *Plato, reincarnation is more generally associated with Eastern religions such as Hinduism. Reincarnation is generally deemed incompatible with the Christian doctrine of *resurrection.

relativism. The theory that denies that humans can possess any objective, universally meaningful knowledge, that there are any ultimate and unchanging *metaphysical realities (God, persons, space, time, natural laws) or that there are any moral absolutes. Hence meaning and truth are relative to each culture and historical period or to each person, situation, relationship and outcome.

Religionsgeschichtliche Schule. German for "history-of-religion school," the influential group of German biblical scholars who between 1880 and 1920 emphasized extensive use of data from comparative studies of other religions to interpret Christianity. Participants in this movement (such as Hermann Gunkel) minimized doctrinal issues in favor of tracing historical, "mythological" developments through Judaism, Christianity and other ancient religions.

Renaissance. French for "rebirth," this term refers to the period of time roughly between 1400 and 1600 during which there was a perceived return to or rebirth of the aesthetic and artistic values of ancient Greece and Rome. The Renaissance entailed a shift from the medieval perception of reality in spiritual terms (with God occupying the central role) to one in which humans were the central figures. Hence this period is often depicted as an era of *humanism. *See also* Erasmus, Desiderius.

resurrection. The central, defining doctrine and claim of the Christian faith is the resurrection of Jesus Christ, whom God brought forth from the dead. The resurrection of the dead refers to the promise based on the bodily resurrection of Jesus, that all believers will one day join Christ in the resurrection. Believers will be transformed, that is, renewed both morally and physically with "spiritual" bodies adapted for eternal life with God.

revelation. Refers both to the process by which God discloses the divine nature and the mystery of the divine will and purpose to human beings, and to the corpus of truth disclosed. Some theologians maintain that revelation consists of both God's activity in *salvation history through word and deed, culminating in Jesus (who mediates and fulfills God's self-revelation) and the ongoing activity of God to move people to yield to, accept and personally appropriate that reality. *General revelation maintains that God's existence and particular attributes can be ascertained through an innate sense of God's reality and conscience as well as through observation of the universe and history. *Special revelation refers to the more specific divine self-disclosure to and through certain persons that brings about human salvation.

revivalism. A historical movement within the church that finds its roots in the *Reformation, *Pietism and English *Puritanism but reached its zenith in the late eighteenth to early twentieth centuries. Revivalism emphasizes the involvement of the emotional as well as the rational dimensions of the human person in a personal event of *conversion as the appropriate response to hearing and receiving the gospel. Revivalism as a type of religious practice often includes mass meetings with gospel music and biblical preaching, and with a strongly emotional appeal for a personal, subjective and public response.

righteousness. An attribute of God's being; God's right and just character, actions and judgments. God's righteousness as understood in a covenantal context includes God's right judgment of both God's own people and those who oppress them, as well as God's *salvation and mercy extended to those to whom the covenanting God has promised to be faithful. Righteousness and salvation are summed up in and provided for all those who believe in the death and *resurrection of Jesus Christ. By extension, righteousness denotes the type of life that ought to characterize Jesus' disciples. Believers are to "imitate" God and thereby become righteous in life just as God is righteous.

Ritschl, Albrecht (1822-1889). A significant German Lutheran theologian often viewed as the paradigm of nineteenth-century Protestant *liberalism. Following the lead of Immanuel *Kant, Ritschl differentiated between scientific knowledge (the attempt to understand reality from a neutral standpoint) and religious knowledge (value judgments about reality). Theology, in turn, is the system of value judgments based on the effects of God on the lives of Christians. Central to Ritschl's theology was the concept of the *kingdom of God. He viewed the church as the community of people who collectively make the value judgment that our highest human good is found in the kingdom of God as revealed in Jesus.

Romanticism. A movement (perhaps better described as an attitude or temperament) within the humanities during the late eighteenth and early nineteenth centuries in reaction to *Enlightenment rationalism and classicism. Romanticism emphasized a subjective, expressive and existential outlook; engagement with the natural, sensual world; and the priority of the imagination over things rational and ordered. Romanticism influenced the theology of Friedrich *Schleiermacher.

S

Sabellianism. An early-third-century trinitarian heresy named for Sabellius, who taught that the one God revealed himself successively in salvation history first as Father (Creator and Lawgiver), then as Son (Redeemer) and finally as Spirit (Sustainer, Giver of Grace). Hence for Sabellius there is only one divine person, not three as in Christian trinitarianism.

sacerdotalism. The emphasis in the Roman Catholic tradition, especially as proclaimed in the Middle Ages, on the powers of earthly priests as essential mediators between God and humankind. Sacerdotalism teaches that by virtue of *ordination priests have the gifting of the Spirit whereby they are able to transform mundane physical elements (water, bread and wine) into means of grace.

sacrament, sacramentalism. Terms used by many Christian traditions to refer to the sacred practices of the church. *Augustine spoke of these acts as "the visible form of an invisible grace" or as a "sign of a sacred thing." Mysteriously, the sacraments are used by God to confirm divine promises to believers and are somehow the means by which the recipient enters into the truths they represent. The two primary sacraments are *baptism and the *Lord's Supper. The lesser sacraments in the Roman Catholic tradition include confirmation, penance, matrimony, ordination (orders) and extreme unction. Protestant theology emphasizes the need for faith in order for a sacrament to have meaning. *Sacramentalism* refers to any understanding of the Christian faith that places high value on the sacraments. More narrowly, *sacramentalism* can be a term used pejoratively of persons or church traditions that see the essence of Christianity as participation in the sacraments rather than as inner transformation and personal piety. *See ex opere operato.*

saints. In the NT, synonymous with the people of God, the church of Jesus Christ. Its OT antecedence implies the idea of being set apart for God as well as conformity to God's likeness through the work of the indwelling Holy Spirit. In the Roman Catholic tradition the saints are persons who have been specially graced by God's Spirit to live in an exemplary manner and to perform special feats. Catholic piety includes veneration of, and prayer to, the saints.

salvation. A broad term referring to God's activity on behalf of creation and especially humans in bringing all things to God's intended goal. More specifically, salvation entails God's deliverance of humans from the power and effects of sin and the *Fall through the work of Jesus Christ so that creation in general and humans in particular can enjoy the fullness of life intended for what God has made.

sanctification. From the Hebrew and Greek, "to be set apart" from common use, "to be made holy." The nature of sanctification is twofold in that Christians have been made holy through Christ and are called to continue to grow into and strive for holiness by cooperating with the indwelling Holy Spirit until they enjoy complete conformity to Christ (*glorification). *See also* Methodism.

satisfaction theory of the atonement. Originating with *Anselm, an understanding of the work of Christ based on the *metaphor of God as a Sovereign who, having been dishonored by sin, must receive satisfaction. Because through sin humans perpetrated the insult, only a human should provide such satisfaction, but the insult was so great that only God can do so. In that he is both God and man, Jesus Christ was able to provide the necessary satisfaction primarily through his obedient death. *See also* atonement.

Schleiermacher, Friedrich (1768-1834). Influential Protestant theologian who attempted to make religion relevant to the German intelligentsia who were steeped in *Romanticism. Schleiermacher emphasized intuition and feeling as the basis of religion (independent of doctrine) and defined religion as the feeling of absolute dependence that finds its highest expression in *monotheism. According to Schleiermacher, Christianity is the highest religion, but in that this feeling may assume diverse individual and cultural religious forms, Christianity may not be the only true religion.

scholasticism. Originally the educational tradition of the medieval schools, but more specifically the method of philosophical and theological reflection set forth most succinctly by Thomas *Aquinas. In attempting to understand better the deep meanings of Christian doctrine, scholasticism aimed to synthesize classical Greek and Roman philosophy with Christian writings and Scripture using Aristotelianism and *Platonism to provide a clear and defined systematic structure. After the *Reformation, certain Protestant theologians continued the scholastic tradition, especially as they came to focus on the quest for right doctrine understood in the form of correct assertions or propositions.

Scripture principle. The Bible read and understood as the Word of God. The Scripture principle, associated with Reformed theologians, holds that the beliefs and practices of the church must be grounded in and derive authority from Scripture.

sect, sectarianism. Originally Latin for "school," or "faction," the term *sect* refers to a subgroup of a larger, usually religious body that is identifiable by its own leadership and teaching and practices. Sects are generally groups that have split off from a larger group or have maintained a unique identity within a larger group. They simply may be unorganized religious movements. Sectarianism is rigid devotion to a sect. In another sense sectarianism refers to the belief that one's own group is the true church in distinction from other groups that are deemed false churches.

secularism, secular humanism. Derived from a word that means simply "belonging to this age," or "worldly," secularism is more specifically the belief system that denies the reality of God, religion and the supernatural order and hence maintains that reality entails only this natural world. Secular humanism in turn promotes and glorifies the human creature to the exclusion and denial of the Creator.

Semi-Pelagianism. A word that later came to be used to describe the doctrines proposed between A.D. 427 and 529 which theologically held a middle ground between Pelagius and *Augustine.

Semi-Pelagians maintain that faith begins independently of God's grace, although such grace is subsequently necessary for *salvation, and that *predestination is simply divine foreknowledge. *See* Pelagianism.

sensus plenior. Latin, meaning the "plenary," or "fuller sense." The *sensus plenior* is the meaning of the Bible as it has come to be interpreted through Christian history while seeking to remain true to the primary sense of what the biblical author meant to convey. The term has also been applied to the manner in which NT writers sometimes reinterpret OT texts.

similitudo Dei. Latin for "likeness of God." Based on a distinction made as early as *Irenaeus between the likeness and the image of God *(see imago Dei)*, some theologians (e.g., *Aquinas) held the likeness to be the supernatural gift of righteousness Adam enjoyed in the Garden but lost in the Fall, in contrast to the natural powers related to the divine image that fallen humans retain. This distinction was rejected by the Reformers.

sin. The fundamental unbelief, distrust and rejection of God and human displacement of God as the center of reality. The Bible presents sin as both fallen humanity's state of separation and alienation from God and as a person's purposeful disobedience to God's will as evidenced in concrete thought or act. As an inherent part of the human condition sin is universal, and it is both corporate and individual.

sinlessness of Christ. The doctrine that Jesus was without sin, free from all transgression of the law and thus able to do the will of the Father in complete holiness. The early debates about Jesus' sinlessness focused on whether his temptations were real, given the *paradox of his being sinless and yet able to be tempted. The question debated was whether Jesus was "able not to sin" (*potuit non peccare*) or "not able to sin" (*non potuit peccare*).

sociology of knowledge. An *epistemological theory that asserts that human knowledge is shaped by social forces. In contrast to the *Enlightenment assumption that knowledge arises as the neutral observer discovers objective truth about the external world, this theory sets forth the idea that knowledge is not neutral or value-free but tends to embody the social circumstances and conditions of the cultural milieu. More important, knowledge tends to reflect the vested interests of the knower.

sola fide. Latin for "faith only," the Lutheran, *Reformation doctrine that the only way to be justified and receive God's grace is through faith, that is, by accepting Christ's merits on one's own behalf.

sola gratia. Latin for "grace only," the Lutheran, *Reformation doctrine that *salvation is God's free gift accomplished by Christ's saving death and *resurrection rather than by human action. *Righteousness, or *justification, comes by God's free gift of grace alone through faith. Roman Catholic doctrine, in contrast, insisted that God requires free human cooperation, although it is God alone who makes such cooperation possible.

sola scriptura. Latin for "Scripture only," the Lutheran, *Reformation principle that Scripture—not Scripture plus church tradition—is the source of Christian revelation. As a result, Scripture is to rule as God's word in the church, unencumbered by papal and ecclesiastical *magisterium (*dogma) and unrivaled by the supposed additional revelation that comes through church tradition.

soteriology. Literally, "the study of *salvation." This topic within the corpus of *systematic theology deals with the work of the triune God in bringing creation, and especially humans, to enjoy the divine purpose for existence. More specifically, "objective" soteriology speaks of the life, death, resurrection and exaltation of Christ in relation to human salvation. In addition, "subjective" soteriology (the work of the Spirit in the application of Christ's salvation) deals with the process whereby individuals are brought to God's saving goals. Topics generally covered include *election, calling, *regeneration, *faith, repentance, conversion, *justification, *sanctification and *glorification.

soul. The spiritual nature, life, being or *essence of the individual human (the unique "person") often thought to survive after death. Theological debates have focused on whether the human person consists of spirit and body in addition to soul, whether the soul is an entity in distinction from the body or whether soul simply refers to the single embodied person as a whole.

source (of theology). Related to theological *norms, the "raw material" involved in theological construction, or that to which theologians appeal in the construction of a systematic delineation of Christian doctrine. Theological sources influence the shape of a theological construction as well as provide its content. *Evangelical theologians appeal to Scripture as the primary source as well as the or norming norm, for theology. Other resources that theologians sometimes propose as theological sources include tradition, reason, culture and experience.

sovereignty. The biblical concept of God's kingly, supreme rule and legal authority over the entire universe. God's sovereignty is expressed, exercised and displayed in the divine plan for and outworking of salvation history. Divine sovereignty is emphasized especially in the Augustinian-Calvinist tradition, where it is paradoxically contrasted with human responsibility.

special revelation. God's divine self-revelation evidenced specifically in salvation history and culminating in the *incarnation as understood through Scripture. Although the Bible seemingly affirms both *general and special revelation (*see* revelation), only special revelation can disclose completely our sinful predicament, as well as God's promise of *salvation and its fulfillment in Christ.

spiration. Literally, "breathing," the term used to describe the way the Spirit proceeds from the Father (and the Son).

Spirit, spirit. Connected with "wind" and "breath," *spirit* refers to life itself, to the life principle and above all to God as the source and giver of life. In addition, the Holy Spirit is the third person of the one triune God and as such is the Life Giver.

spirituality, Christian. The believer's relationship with God and life in the Spirit as a member of the church of Jesus Christ. Today spirituality often refers to an interest in or concern for matters of the "spirit" in contrast to the mere interest and focus on the material. Christian spirituality in turn entails a desire to allow one's Christian commitment to shape every dimension of life. Some see Christian spirituality as expressed through participation in certain Christian practices, such as Bible study, prayer, worship and so forth.

structuralism, structuralist exegesis. A broad movement in literary *criticism incorporating several different approaches, structuralism contends that meaning is the product of "deep structures"—basic, universal ways of understanding and articulating things—that are found in the text. Structuralism seeks to identify and classify these structures and then use them to assist in interpretation.

subjectivism. The theory or doctrine that limits knowledge to personal (or perhaps even private) experience. What is supremely good and right can only be ascertained by individual feeling or apprehension.

sublapsarianism, infralapsarianism. Related to a debate among Calvinists over the intricacies of divine election, this position asserts that God's decree of *election logically follows God's decree to allow the *Fall of humankind into sin. That is, the decree of election is "sublapsarian" in contrast to "supralapsarian," which places this decree prior to the decree to allow the Fall. Consequently, sublapsarians view *election as God's predetermined, willed response to the Fall. *See also* supralapsarianism.

subordinationism. A second- and third-century *heresy that held that because the Son and the Spirit proceed from the Father, they are not equal to the Father and are thus not fully divine.

substantia. Latin for "substance," referring to *essence or essential nature. The matter of the *substantia* of God was a primary issue in patristic and medieval developments of the doctrine of Christ and the *Trinity.

Summa Theologica (**Summa**). Latin for a "summary of theology," the phrase more specifically refers to the major systematic theology of Thomas *Aquinas.

summum bonum. A Latin phrase referring to the "supreme good" from which all other good is derived. In medieval theology the human supreme good was depicted as the "beatific vision," the contemplation of the eternal *essence of God.

supralapsarianism. A *Calvinistic view of *predestination that maintains that in the "logical order of divine decrees" God decreed the *election of some persons and the reprobation of others before allowing the *Fall of Adam. Hence the *decree of election is "supralapsarian." In supralapsarianism the emphasis is on God's *predestination of uncreated and unfallen humans rather than on created and fallen humanity (sublapsarianism). Consequently the supralapsarian view leads to the idea of double predestination: God has chosen to glorify himself by predestining certain persons to eternal life and others to eternal condemnation. *See also* sublapsarianism, infralapsarianism.

syncretism. The attempt to assimilate differing or opposite doctrines and practices, especially between philosophical and religious systems, resulting in a new system altogether in which the fundamental structure and tenets of each have been changed. Syncretism of the gospel occurs when its essential character is confused with elements from the culture. In syncretism the gospel is lost as the church simply confirms what is already present in the culture.

Synod of Dort. The assembly (synod) of the Dutch Reformed Church convened at Dort in 1618-1619 to deal primarily with the issues of separation of church and state and the Arminian controversy. The synod was biased against *Arminianism and produced the Canons of Dort, which upheld the doctrines of the total depravity of humankind, unconditional *election, *limited atonement, the irresistibility of divine grace and the final *perseverance (or God's preservation) of the saints. *See also* Calvinism, John Calvin; TULIP.

Synoptic Gospels, synoptic problem. The Synoptic Gospels are Matthew, Mark and Luke, which reflect many similarities to each other, in contrast to John's Gospel, which provides a quite different (albeit complementary) picture of Jesus. The synoptic problem centers around the literary relation and interdependence among the three Gospels based on their shared subject matter and frequent textual similarities.

systematic theology. The attempt to summarize religious truth or the belief system of a religious group (such as Christianity) through an organized system of thought carried out within a particular cultural and intellectual context (*see* method of theology). A common systematic order in Christian theology begins with God and God's self-revelation, followed by creation and the predicament of sin, God's saving work in and through Jesus Christ, the Spirit as the agent in personal *salvation, the church as the redeemed community of God's people, and finally the goal of God's program as leading to the end of the age, Christ's return and eternity.

T

teleological argument. An argument for the existence of God based on the seemingly purposeful order of the universe that suggests the world is the work of a "Master Architect" rather than a result of chance. Important proponents of teleological arguments include the medieval theologian Thomas *Aquinas and the *Enlightenment apologist William Paley (1743-1805).

Tertullian (A.D. 160-220). Next to *Augustine perhaps the greatest Western theologian of the *patristic period. Tertullian was one of the first major Christian theologians to write in Latin (the language of Western theology) and authored many apologetic, theological and controversial works in defense of Christianity. Tertullian is often credited as being the first important theologian to use the term *Trinity,* describing God as "one substance in three persons."

theism. The system of belief that presupposes the reality of God as the foundational concept informing all other beliefs. Any worldview anchored in the belief that there is a God.

theistic evolutionism. An understanding of the development of life on earth that arose out of the attempt to relate the interpretation of Genesis to the scientific theory of organic evolution by taking a nonliteral view of the creation account while wholeheartedly trusting its truthfulness as the Word of God. Theistic evolution teaches that while the various species emerged through the evolutionary process, God superintended the development of life. That is, evolution was the means that God used in bringing about the divine purpose of creating life on this planet. Theistic evolutionists generally maintain the classical Christian doctrines of creation, original sin and human depravity in need of redemption.

theocentricity. Holding God as the central object of focus and interest as well as our ultimate concern. Hence, to be theocentric is to view all of life, including *ethics, from the perspective of a commitment to God.

theodicy. A response to the problem of evil in the world that attempts logically, relevantly and consistently to defend God as simultaneously omnipotent, all-loving and just despite the reality of evil.

theologia crucis, theologia gloriae. In his *theologia crucis* (theology of the cross) Luther contended that the true and consummate place of God's self-revelation is in the humility, weakness and suffering love of God displayed on the cross of Christ. Luther opposed the idea of a *theologia gloriae* (theology of glory) that advocated the knowledge of God through God's works in the cosmos.

theological method. *See* method in theology, methodology.

theology. A religious belief system about God or ultimate reality. *Theology* commonly refers to the ordered, systematic study or interpretation of the Christian faith and experience of God based on God's divine self-revelation. Theology also seeks to apply these truths to the full breadth of human experience and thought.

theology of hope. An *eschatological approach to theology originating in Germany in the 1960s and associated most often with Jürgen Moltmann (1926-). The theology of hope views the future as already begun in the present based on the hope and promise generated by Christ's *resurrection. As a result, the church is to be a people of hope who experience God in the present through God's promises, who maintain a corporate rather than merely a private understanding of *salvation and who confront the present age with a vision of transformation.

theopneustos. Greek for "God-breathed," or "God-inspired." Generally this word is used to describe the divine dimension of Scripture either as divinely inspired documents (see 2 Tim 3:16) or as the product of divinely inspired authors (2 Pet 1:21).

third use of the law. The addition of a third purpose for the divine law beyond its role in suppressing human wickedness and acting as a "schoolmaster" leading sinful humans to Christ. In its third use the law provides direction for believers along the pathway of *sanctification. Whereas the *Lutheran tradition tends to focus on the first two uses, *Reformed theologians also give place to the third, which leads to a stronger emphasis on sanctification as growth in obedience to the divine law.

Thirty-Nine Articles, the. The set of doctrinal formulas (short summaries of doctrinal tenets) presenting the formal position of the Church of England (as of 1563) in response to and in the context of the key controversies of the English Reformation in the sixteenth century.

Thomism, neo-Thomism. Thomism refers to the teachings of Thomas *Aquinas and the subsequent philosophical and theological schools that were based on his thought. The twentieth-century revival of Thomism, known as neo-Thomism, took two major forms: transcendental Thomism (represented by Karl Rahner and Bernard Lonergan) accommodates the major concerns of Thomism with insights from Immanuel *Kant, whereas neoscholastic Thomism (represented by Etienne Gilson and Jacques Maritain) seeks to recover and reaffirm a "pure version" of Aquinas's original teachings.

Tillich, Paul (1886-1965). One of the most influential Protestant theologians of the twentieth century, Tillich developed a philosophical theology to respond to and seriously interact with modern culture. Best known for his *method of correlation, Tillich argued that all reality—including God, the Ground of Being—can be known only through myth and symbol. By participating in the Ground of Being as revealed by the "New Being," humans can move from fallen "nonbeing" into new, human "being," whose perfect symbol is Jesus the Christ.

time, timelessness. *Time* refers to the relation of events within creation to each other. Generally events are viewed as forming a linear succession, leading to the idea of the "time line." But the succession of events might also be cyclical, resulting in time as a circle. The Bible presents time as a divinely created reality in which God historically works out the divine plan of *salvation. Thus time begins "in the beginning" and moves linearly toward a future goal. Philosophers and theologians have debated how time and eternity are related, as well as the nature of the connection between God and time. Some thinkers assert that time and eternity are totally distinct, while others collapse them, in part as a reaction against viewing time as itself being an entity. Theologians who assert that God is timeless maintain that God created time and therefore stands "above" the temporal flow. Others suggest that God travels with creation through time.

tradition, traditionalism. Among the early Christian fathers, *tradition* (meaning something "handed over") meant the revelation of God made known to people through the prophets and apostles. Eventually the term came to mean the Scripture and *creeds, and still later it included the accumulated explanations of the faith and wisdom of the church though history. In reaction to eighteenth-century rationalism, certain nineteenth-century Roman Catholic thinkers upheld the idea that knowledge of God could only be attained through faith in revealed, unbroken and infallible tradition (traditionalism) as opposed to such means as *natural theology and human reason.

traducianism. The view that in addition to the human body the human soul is transmitted from the parents to the child, rather than being created specifically for that human body by God *ex nihilo* (*creationism). Although it may be dated to the patristic era, this teaching has been especially strong in Lutheran circles, in contrast to the Roman Catholic and Reformed preference for creationism.

transcendence. The attribute of God that refers to being wholly and distinctly separate from creation (although always actively involved in and with it as well). The declaration that God is transcendent means that God is "above" the world and comes to creation from "beyond." During the medieval era God's transcendence was especially emphasized, as is evident in the architecture of the great gothic cathedrals with their high, arched ceilings that lift one's gaze upward.

transcendental philosophy, theology. A philosophy that emphasizes the transcendent as the fundamental reality, that seeks to identify the preconditions for human knowledge and experience, and that embraces the ultimate unknowability of ultimate reality. Transcendental theology assumes that humans are transcendent (spirit as well as matter) in that they are oriented toward an infinite, mysterious horizon of being (God) and thus open to and receptive of divine revelation.

transubstantiation. A term in Roman Catholic theology meaning "essential change," the belief that by the power of God at the consecration in the Mass, the bread and wine change substance into the actual substance of Jesus' body and blood, even though they seem to retain their natural characteristics.

tribulation. The internal and external suffering of God's people which, according to NT teaching, followers of Jesus Christ are to expect as a matter of course. The NT references to the "great tribulation" describe an unprecedented period of global suffering that will mark the time just prior to the *parousia. Different millennial views place the time of the tribulation at different points in relation to the *millennium. Likewise, different views on the time of the *rapture place this event at different points in relation to the *eschatological tribulation.

trichotomism. An understanding of human nature as divided into three parts: body, soul and spirit (e.g., 1 Thess 5:23; Heb 4:12). According to trichotomists, the spirit, the part of a human being that is capable of knowing God, is to be differentiated from the soul, which is the seat of the personality. Often numbered among trichotomists are the church father *Irenaeus and the nineteenth-century biblical scholar Franz Delitzsch. The viewpoint can be found as well in the Scofield Reference Bible.

Trinity. The Christian understanding of God as triune. Trinity means that the one divine nature is a unity of three persons and that God is revealed as three distinct persons: Father, Son and Holy Spirit. The ultimate basis for the Christian doctrine of the Trinity lies in the divine self-disclosure in Jesus, who as the Son revealed the Father and poured out the Holy Spirit. *See also* economic Trinity; immanent Trinity.

tritheism. A distorted belief in three different Gods—Father, Son and Spirit—rather than one God who is unified and yet diversely three persons (*Trinity).

truth. That which reflects factual and/or spiritual reality. Some thinkers view truth in purely intellectual categories, namely, as the affirmation of what is. Hence truth becomes correct assertions or factual statements (factuality). In recent times certain thinkers have suggested that truth is subjective, relative and pluralistic. Viewed from a theological perspective, truth is grounded in the being and will of the triune God. Hence whatever reflects God's own being and will is truth. Furthermore, Jesus Christ is the truth in that he is the *revelation of God.

TULIP. An acronym referring to the five theological tenets affirmed at the *Synod of Dort (total *depravity, unconditional *election, *limited atonement, irresistible grace, the *perseverance [or divine preservation] of the saints). Since then, this acronym has come to be used as a summary of the teaching of Calvinism. *See also* Calvinism, John Calvin.

two natures, doctrine of. A way of describing the orthodox position about the person of Christ as being fully human and fully divine. Upheld at the *Council of Ephesus (A.D. 431) and clarified at the Council of Chalcedon (A.D. 451), the two-natures doctrine affirms that the one person Jesus Christ is both divine and human. In the incarnation the two natures became united in one person. As a result, the two form a *hypostasis (that is, they do not merely exist side by side), although they remain distinct (that is, they are not coalesced or changed into a composite third nature).

typology. Differing from a symbol or an allegory, a typology is a representation of an actual, historical reference. According to Christian exegesis, biblical typology deals with the parallels between actual, historical (usually OT) figures or events in *salvation history and their later, analogous fulfillment. Often NT events and figures are typologically understood and interpreted according to an OT pattern (e.g., creation and the new creation, Adam and Christ, the exodus and NT concepts of salvation). On this basis typology became one of the four prevalent ways (together with the literal, the analogical and the spiritual) of interpreting Scripture in the Middle Ages.

U

ubiquity, ubiquitarianism. The doctrine developed by Luther and maintained by many of his followers that Christ in his human nature is present everywhere. Lutherans appeal to the doctrine of the ubiquity of Christ to support the belief that Christ is physically present in the *eucharistic elements (the *real presence), in contrast to *Reformed thinkers (e.g., *Zwingli) who argue that the physical Jesus is localized at the right hand of the Father in heaven and therefore cannot be present in the bread and the wine.

ultimate concern. The idea arising from Paul *Tillich that everyone has something that is of highest importance to him or her. Tillich suggested that persons' ultimate concern, or "what concerns ultimately," is their God. In this sense, everyone is inherently religious.

unconditional election. The view (common among *Calvinists) that *election, understood as the predetermination of the destiny of human individuals, is based on God's sovereign, eternal *decree rather than merely on divine foreknowledge of whether they will freely reject or accept *salvation through Jesus Christ (as is generally taught by *Arminians).

Unitarianism. Also referred to as antitrinitarianism, Unitarianism's roots are the *Arian denial of the doctrine of the *Trinity (thus asserting that the Father begat the Son at a point in time so that the Son is not eternal). Modern, humanistic Unitarianism reflects the influences of the *Enlightenment and nineteenth-century transcendentalism in its further rejection of the authority of Scripture and of the supernatural. Modern Unitarians generally speak of Jesus as an ethical ideal, a great moral teacher or even a messenger from God. But in Unitarian thought Jesus cannot be the eternal Son of the eternal Father, because God is one, not three persons.

universalism. Known historically as *apokatastasis,* the belief that all persons will be saved. Hence universalism involves the affirmation of universal *salvation and the denial of eternal punishment. Universalists believe that ultimately all humans are somehow in union with Christ and that in the fullness of time they will gain release from the penalty of sin and be restored to God. Twentieth-century universalism often rejects the deity of Jesus and explores the "universal" bases of all religions. *See also apokatastasis.*

univocal. The idea that a word carries the same meaning when applied to God that it has when predicated of something in creation. Thus human fatherhood and divine Fatherhood are identical ideas. The univocal use of language ignores God's distinctiveness and uniqueness from creation. *See* equivocal.

V

Vatican, Vatican Council. Literally, an enclave within the city of Rome, the Vatican forms the residence of the pope. Figuratively, a reference to the pope or to papal, magisterial authority. Its present common usage also refers to the Second Vatican Council (Vatican II: 1962-1965), which sought to bring all aspects of Roman Catholic faith and life into harmony with contemporary concerns or the modern age.

vestigium trinitatis. Latin for "vestiges of the *Trinity" (most likely originating with *Augustine), the drawing of analogies to the Trinity from the threefold related structure of certain created things. For example, Augustine saw a vestige of the Trinity in the human person, one's self-knowledge and one's self-love.

vestigium Dei. Latin for "vestiges of God," the view that there are vestiges, or evidences, of the one God in the created order and that God has revealed the divine being analogously in creation.

via eminentiae, via negativa, via causalitatus. Latin for the "way of eminence," the *via eminentiae* or *via analogiae* (way of analogy) refers to *Aquinas's analogical approach to the understanding of and language about God. Aquinas considered all speech about God analogous in that it uses finite images from creation that allow the theologian to make positive though inadequate affirmations of God. Through the *via negativa* "negative" statements (saying what God is not) are used to articulate the ineffability of God (e.g., incomprehensibility and infallibility). Aquinas's analogical predication depends on an interpretation of the doctrine of creation that sees all things as brought into being and sustained by God, who is the cause of the world, causality itself being an analogical notion. Thus the *via causalitatus* allows the theologian to predicate of God all that must be said about God as the first cause of the world.

via media. The idea (popularized by John Henry Newman in

nineteenth-century Britain) that the *Anglican Church represented a "middle way" between Roman Catholicism and the modernizing elements (both *liberal and *evangelical) of Protestantism.

vicarious (atonement). Literally, "in place of." Hence in that Jesus died "for us," that is, took on himself the consequences of human sin, theologians often speak of his sacrificial, substitutionary death as a *vicarious* atonement.

virgin birth (virginal conception). The doctrine that holds that the Holy Spirit without the participation of a human father conceived Jesus in the womb of Mary.

visible church. The church as an organization that encompasses baptized members of local congregations, in contrast to the *invisible church, which includes all true believers (or elect persons) and therefore is known only to God. Alternately, the church as consisting of those who are now living, in contrast to the invisible company of saints who have died and are now present in heaven with God.

voluntarism. A philosophical and theological view that opposes rationalism and elevates the place and function of human will (in contrast to reason) in the attainment of truth and moral good. The word *voluntarism* is also used to refer to the idea that the church is made up of believers who voluntarily join together and covenant together to walk with one another as the people of God.

Vulgate. The Latin translation of the Bible completed by Jerome (c. 347-420), which was declared the "official edition" for the Roman Catholic Church at the *Council of Trent (1546).

W

Wesleyanism, John Wesley (1703-1791). The various groups and churches associated with, spawned by or that look for their genesis in John Wesley (the founder of *Methodism) and his theology. These include the various Methodist churches, the *Holiness Movement and *Pentecostalism. Wesley's theology attempted to balance the doctrine of *justification by faith with an emphasis on the Spirit's ongoing process of *sanctification in the life of the believer. Wesleyans are often known for certain doctrines, including entire sanctification and the second blessing. Wesleyans tend to be *Arminian as opposed to *Calvinist in their understanding of the dynamic of personal *salvation.

Wesleyan quadrilateral. The four "sources" on which Wesleyan theology is often constructed and defended: Scripture, reason, tradition and experience. There is some debate today as to whether the Wesleyan quadrilateral actually dates to Wesley himself, although there is general agreement that it does represent Wesley's own theological approach.

Westminster Confession and Catechisms. The confession commissioned (and subsequently rejected) by the English Parliament to help give a Puritan structure to the Church of England. The Westminster Confession (completed in 1646) is the most influential of the Reformed confessions in the English-speaking world, having been adopted by the British and American Presbyterian denominations and certain Baptist and Congregational denominations. The (Larger and Shorter) Westminster Catechisms follow the theology of the Confession and are used for official doctrinal teaching within the Reformed tradition.

will of God. God's divine purpose for creation as a whole and for human beings in particular. Many theologians distinguish between God's "free" will and God's "necessary" will. God's will is free in that as Creator God acts toward creation out of freedom rather than compulsion, but God's will is necessary in that God always acts in a manner consistent with the divine nature or character. Theologians likewise sometimes differentiate between God's "hidden" will (what God alone knows he will do) and God's "revealed" will (what God discloses to humans about what he will do or purposes that creatures do).

Word of God. Encompassing the OT meaning of what God speaks, especially through prophetic spokespersons, the Christian meaning refers first to God's self-revelation in Jesus Christ as the Word (e.g., Jn 1:1). It also refers to the proclamation of the gospel of Christ and by extension to the Scriptures that testify to the truth of Christ.

worship. The act of adoring and praising God, that is, ascribing worth to God as the one who deserves homage and service. The church, which is to be a worshiping community (1 Pet 2:5), expresses its worship corporately and publicly (*liturgically) through prayer; through psalms, hymns and spiritual songs; through the reading and exposition of Scripture; through observance of the *sacraments; and through individual and corporate living in holiness and service.

wrath of God. The free, subjective and holy response of God to sin and to the evil and wickedness exhibited by creatures in opposition to God.

X, Y, Z

Zwingli, Ulrich (1484-1531). The leader of the Swiss Reformation, Zwingli is often numbered with Luther and Calvin as one of the most influential Protestant Reformers. A strict adherent to the biblical text, Zwingli rejected Luther's position of *consubstantiation in regard to the presence of Christ in the *Eucharist, arguing instead for a *memorialist view. Zwingli inspired but later broke with the developing *Anabaptist movement.